CUSTOMS ACT- SUPREME COURT'S LEADING CASE LAWS

CASE NOTES- FACTS- FINDINGS OF APEX COURT JUDGES & CITATIONS

JAYPRAKASH BANSILAL SOMANI

ISBN 979-888591812-1

Dedicated

To

All the Past & Present Judges of the Supreme Court of India.

Salute to their wisdom.

Salute to their interpretation of Law.

Salute to their elaborative judgement writing.

ꙮ

Contents

Contents

PREFACE

Dear Learned Advocates of the Trial Courts, Tribunals, High Courts, Supreme Court, & Individuals

I am very delighted to provide you a book on 'CUSTOMS ACT'- Supreme Court of India's Leading Case Laws'.

In this book you will get...

1. Name of the Case i. e. Cause title

2.Relevant Sections discussed in the case

3. Hon'ble Judges/Coram of the case

4.Number of PDF Pages in Original Judgement of the case

5. All available Citations of the case

6. Case Note with appeal allowed/ dismissed or disposed off

7. Facts of the case

8. Hon'ble Apex Court's findings, while dismissing/allowing or disposing the appeal

9. Ratio Decidendi if any.

My special thanks to Manupatra, because of their web portal I can compile this book in well manner. I am also thankful to Notion Press to support me to publish & market this book throughout the Country. Thanks to my Juniors, Advocate Colleagues & Insolvency Professional Colleagues to support me in this venture.

Mr Rachit Manchanda has helped me a lot to compile this book.

I hope this book will add some value addition in the wealth of your legal knowledge. Your positive feedbacks will boost me to compile/ write further books & negative feedbacks will improve my skills. Kindly send your valuable feedbacks by email.

Thanks with Regards,

Jayprakash B. Somani

Advocate, Supreme Court of India

Email: jaysomani64@gmail.com

Web Site:www.jayprakashsomani.com

Call: 8384051134, 9322188701, 9318381287

ACKNOWLEDGEMENTS

Printed & Published by
Notion Press
No. 8, 3rd Cross Street,
CIT Colony, Mylapore,
Chennai, Tamil Nadu- 600004

Managed by
Jayprakash Somani Advocates & Solicitors
Law Firm for Supreme Court of India
Delhi Office
257 C, Pocket 1, Mayur Vihar Phase 1, Delhi 110091.
Call 8384051134, 9322188701, 8459194576, 9318381287 01141051516
Supreme Court Chamber
312, 3rd Floor, M. C. Setalvad Block, In front of 'D' Gate, Bhagwan Das Road, Supreme Court of India, New Delhi 110001
Contact: 8459194576, 9811011747,
www.jayprakashsomani.com

Books are available online at
1. **Notion Press:** https://notionpress.com/author/jayprakash_somani
2. **Amazon:** https://www.amazon.in/s?k=jayprakash+somani
3. **Flipkart:** https://www.flipkart.com/search?q=Jayprakash%20Somani

I

The Trustees of the Port of Madras Vs. Aminchand Pyarelal and Ors., 1975

Hon'ble Judges/Coram: A.N. Ray, C.J., K.K. Mathew and Y.V. Chandrachud, JJ.

Relevant Section:

Customs Act, 1962 - Section 111(a), Section 17

Equivalent Citation: AIR1975SC1935, (1976)3SCC167, [1976]1SCR721, MANU/SC/0235/1975

No. of pages in Original Judgement: 10

Case Note:

Customs - demurrage charges - Indian Contract Act, 1872 - whether respondents liable to pay demurrage demanded by appellant - appellant suffered loss due to negligence of respondent - Collector of Customs cannot be held personally liable - appellant was in position to avoid loss in question had he taken proper care - appellant avoided consequences flowing from certificate.

Brief facts of the case:

The Trustees of the Port of Madras, appellants herein, filed Suit No. 158 of 1966 in the High Court of Madras for recovering a sum of Rs. 3,18,968.04 from the respondents by way of demurrage. The 1st respondent is a firm called M/s. Aminchand Pyare lal. the 2nd respondent is the Union of India and the 3rd respondent is the Collector of Customs, Madras. A learned single Judge referred the suit to a Division Bench which dismissed it by a judgment dated December 23, 1971. This is an appeal by certificate granted by the High Court under Article 133(1)(a) of the Constitution.

On April 10, 1963, a Steamer "A. P. J. AKASH" arrived at the Madras Port and landed, among other goods, a consignment of 202 bundles of black plain sheets of various sizes. The appellants received the goods and stored them in transit sheds. The goods were Imported by the 1st respondent under an authorisation issued by the State Trading Corporation of India which held a licence dated June 16, 1962, to import the goods from Hungary. The Clearing Agents of the 1st respondent filed a Bill of Entry with the 3rd respondent but the Customs authorities detained the goods as the specifications in the import licence did not tally with the description of the imported goods. The Customs authorities then issued a show cause notice to the 1st respondent and after considering its explanation the 3rd respondent passed an Order on November 12, 1963, confiscating the goods under Section 111(a) of the Customs Act, 1962. The 1st respondent preferred an appeal against that Order to the Central Board of Excise and Customs New Delhi, which was allowed by the Board on July 27, 1954. On August 21, 1964. the Clearing Agents of the 1st respondent requested the Customs Authorities to issue a certificate for the remission of the transit dues for the period during which the goods were detained. A certificate was accordingly issued by the 3rd respondent stating that the goods were detained by the Customs Authorities from April 24, 1963, to August 21, 1964 for examination under Section 17(3) and Section 17(4) of the Customs Act 1962. other than in the ordinary process of appraisement and that the detention was due to no fault or negligence on the part of the 1st respondent. Acting on this certificate, appellants waived the demurrage for the period covered by the certificate, whereupon the 1st respondent cleared the consignment on August 25 and August 27, 1964. on payment of the Harbour dues. Carnage charges and Demurrage charges for the period not covered by the certificate.

Held,

The High Court was therefore in error in holding the scale of rates fix ed by the Board as ultra vires and void on the grounds that it is unreasonable and that it is in excess of the power conferred by 42 of the Act.

The only question which now remains to be considered is whether the respondents are liable to pay the demur rage demanded of them by the appellants. The appellants' claim against respondents 2 and 3 has no foundation in law and was rightly not pressed by the appellants' counsel. Respondent 3 is the Collector of Customs who. Obviously, cannot be made personally liable to pay the demurrage. Respondent 2 is the Union of India against whom and respondent 3, the appellant's claim is said to reside partly in the region of "contract or quasi-contract". We are unable to spell out any such basis on which the claim of the appellants could rest. The issuance of an incorrect 'Detention Certificate' by the 3rd respondent cannot also help the appellants to fasten the liability for demurrage on respondents 2 and 3 on the ground of their negligence. As observed by the High Court, all the relevant facts were before the appellants who could, with reasonable care have avoided the consequences flowing from the Certificate issued by the 3rd respondent. As regards the appellants' claim against the 1st respondent, the High Court was prepared to hold the latter liable to pay the demurrage except for the fact that the scale of rates was unreasonable and beyond the power of the Board. As we have set aside the High Court's findings on those points, it has to be examined whether the 1st respondent is liable to pay the demurrage. Unfortunately, parties fought in the High Court a legal battle and gave no importance to facts on which the liability of the 1st respondent may be said to rest. Facts must come before the law for, legal principles cannot be applied in a vacuum. No oral evidence was led by the parties and we find it difficult on a mere perusal of documents to say that respondent 1 ought to be held liable to meet the appellants' claim. Documents do not prove themselves nor indeed is the admissibility of a document proof by itself of the truth of its contents Import Licence No. CL/53/ 3/02105-1 dated June 16, 1962, under which the goods were imported stood in the name of the State Trading Corporation of India. It issued an authorisation in favour of the 1st respondent which, as the documents go, was liable to deliver the consignment to the nominees of the Corporation. The 1st respondent, it would appear, was only entitled to charge a Commission for the work done by it in pursuance of the authorisation issued by the Corporation. The 1st respondent had no title to or interest in the goods except to deliver them in accordance with the instructions of the Corporation. If the appellants were to enforce their statutory lien, the incidence of the demurrage would have fallen on the Corporation in whom the title to the Roods was Vested. The appellants permitted the goods to be cleared without then demanding the demurrage which they claimed later, thereby depriving the 1st respondent of an opportunity to reject the goods as against the supplier unless, of course, the Corporation was willing to accept them and along with them the liability for the payment of demurrage. In the absence of any more facts we find it impossible, on the record as it stands, to accept the appellants' claim against the 1st respondent. Out of 15 issues framed in the suit, issues 1 and 10 only pertain to the liability of the 1st respondent and on those issues, the facts appearing on the record are too scanty to support the appellants' claim against the 1st respondent. We, therefore, hold that the claim against the 1st respondent must also fail. 35. In the result, we confirm the decree of the High Court dismissing the appellants' suit, though for entirely different reasons. In the circumstances, there will be no Order as to costs.

II

The Chairman, Board of Trustees, Cochin Port Trust Vs. Arebee Star Maritime Agencies Pvt. Ltd. and Ors., 2018

Hon'ble Judges/Coram: R.K. Agrawal and Dr. D.Y. Chandrachud, JJ.

Acts/Rules/Orders:

Major Port Trusts Act, 1963 - Section 2, Section 3, Section 5, Section 35, Section 42, Section 42(2), Section 42(7), Section 43, Section 43(1), Section 47A, Section 48, Section 49, Section 49A, Section 49B, Section 49(1), Section 50, Section 50B, Section 50B, Section 59, Section 59(1), Section 60, Section 60(1), Section 61, Section 62, Section 63; Customs Act, 1962 - Section 48, Section 150; Indian Bills of Lading Act, 1856 - Section 1; Madras Port Trust Act, 1905 - Section 39, Section 40; Indian Contract Act, 1872 - Section 148, Section 151, Section 152, Section 158, Section 161

Equivalent Citation: 2018(360)ELT3(S.C.), 2018(3)SCALE685, (2018)4SCC592, MANU/SC/0223/2018

No. of pages in Original Judgement: 10

Case Note:

Civil - Ground rent - Liability thereof - Synthetic woollen rags in Port Trust premises was imported - Said containers were destuffed to facilitate

Customs examination and to return empty containers to Steamer Agents - Destuffed cargo occupied much larger space and was not promptly cleared by consignees in view of hurdles placed by Customs stating that cargo actually did not constitute old woollen rags as declared, but mostly were brand new clothes which could not have been cleared - Consignees did not turn up to clear goods and they were lying idle in Port premises for quite long - Port Trust charged ground rent from Steamer Agents/owners of containers - High Court held that there was no justification for Port Trust to collect ground rent charges in respect of containers indefinitely - Hence, present appeal - Whether liability to pay ground rent on containers unloaded at Port could be imposed on owners of vessel/steamer agents beyond period of seventy five days.

Brief Facts of the case:

The synthetic woollen rags (in containers) was imported in the Port Trust premises. The said containers were destuffed to facilitate Customs examination and to return the empty containers to the Steamer Agents. The destuffed cargo occupied much larger space and was not promptly cleared by the consignees in view of the hurdles placed by the Customs stating that the cargo actually did not constitute old woollen rags as declared, but mostly were brand new clothes which could not have been cleared. The modus operandi of the consignees/importers attracted wide attention of all concerned and taking note of the probable extent of liability to be imposed by the Customs Department, and the liability to be satisfied to the Port and others concerned, the consignees did not turn up to clear the goods and they were lying idle in the Port premises for quite long. The Port Trust charged ground rent' from the Steamer Agents/owners of the containers. The High Court held that there was no justification for the Port Trust to collect 'ground rent' charges in respect of the containers indefinitely. The High Court rejected the contention of the Port Trust, that there was no obligation cast upon it, to have destuffed the goods when the containers landed.

Held,

Taking note of the above inconsistencies in the judgments which have been delivered after the pronouncement by the Constitution Bench in **Rowther-I**, we are inclined to the view that the following issues need to be resolved by a larger Bench:

a) Whether in the interpretation of the provision of Section 2(o) of the MPT Act, the question of title of goods, and the point of time at which title passes to the consignee is relevant to determine the liability of the consignee or steamer agent in respect of charges to be paid to the Port Trust;

b) Whether a consignor or a steamer agent is absolved of the responsibility to pay charges due to a Port Trust, for its services in respect of goods which are not cleared by the consignee, once the Bill of lading is endorsed or the delivery order is issued;

c) Whether a steamer agent can be made liable for payment of storage charges/demurrage, etc. in respect of goods which are not cleared by the consignee, where the steamer agent has not issued a delivery order; if so, to what extent;

d) What are the principles which determine whether a Port Trust is entitled to recover its dues, from the steamer agent or the consignee; and

e) While the Port Trust does have certain statutory obligations with regard to the goods entrusted to it, whether there is any obligation, either statutory or contractual, that obliges the Port Trust to de-stuff every container that is entrusted to it and return the empty containers to the shipping agent.

The larger Bench may deal with any additional issues relevant to the context, as it deems necessary.

We request the Registry to place the papers before the Hon'ble Chief Justice of India for such administrative directions as may be considered appropriate

III

L.R. Brothers Indo Flora Ltd. Vs. Commissioner of Central Excise, 2020

Hon'ble Judges/Coram: A.M. Khanwilkar and Dinesh Maheshwari, JJ.

Relevant Section:

Customs Act, 1962 - Section 12; Section 28

Equivalent Citation: 2020(373)ELT721(S.C.), MANU/SC/0664/2020

No. of pages in Original Judgement: 16

Case Note:

Customs - Sale of flowers - Levy of duty - Appellant engaged in production of cut flowers and flower buds of all kinds, suitable for bouquets and for ornamental purposes - Appellant made DTA sales in contravention of provisions of EXIM Policy - Additional Commissioner issued show cause notice to Appellant to show cause as to why customs duty, interest and penalty should not be imposed for DTA sales made by Appellant in contravention of EXIM Policy - Additional Commissioner held that DTA sales were made without permission of Development Commissioner and in contravention of EXIM Policy and therefore, customs duty was leviable upon Appellant for said sales - Appellant unsuccessfully carried matter in appeal before Commissioner wherein Order-in-Original came to be confirmed - Matter was further carried in appeal before Appellate Tribunal - Appellate Tribunal confirmed customs duty levied upon Appellant on sale of cut flowers within Domestic Tariff Area - Hence, present appeal - Whether customs duty could be charged on non-excisable goods and amendment in terms of Notification was prospective or retrospective in its application.

Brief Facts of the case:

The Appellant was engaged in production of cut flowers and flower buds of all kinds, suitable for bouquets and for ornamental purposes. The EOU was required to export all articles produced by it. As a consequence whereof, it was exempted from payment of customs duty on the imported inputs used during production of the exported articles, vide Notification. The Appellant, without obtaining the approval of the Development Commissioner and without maintaining the requisite net foreign exchange earning, made DTA sales in contravention of the provisions of EXIM Policy. The Additional Commissioner issued a show cause notice to the Appellant to show cause as to why customs duty, interest and penalty should not be imposed for the DTA sales made by the Appellant in contravention of the EXIM Policy, that too after having availed the exemptions under the exemption notification on the import of green house equipment, raw materials like Live Rose Plants and consumables like planting materials and fertilizers. After according opportunity of being heard, the Additional Commissioner adjudged the show cause notice and held that the DTA sales were made without permission of the Development Commissioner and in contravention of the EXIM Policy and therefore, customs duty was leviable upon the Appellant for the said sales. The Appellant unsuccessfully carried the matter in appeal before the Commissioner wherein the Order-in-Original came to be confirmed. The matter was further carried in appeal before Appellate Tribunal. The Appellate Tribunal confirmed the customs duty levied upon the Appellant on the sale of cut flowers within the Domestic Tariff Area.

Held,

Applying the afore quoted dictum to the present case, the Appellant was obliged to comply with the conditions prescribed by the EXIM Policy, to avail the exemption under the stated notification; and failure to do so, must denude them of the exemption so granted. Further, since the charging rate prescribed under the exemption notification is under question, any ambiguity in regard to the date of application of the amendment thereto would necessarily have to be construed in favour of the State, unless shown otherwise by judicially acceptable parameters.

The next contention of the Appellant is that Section 28 of the 1962 Act cannot be invoked to extend the limitation as there was no wilful mis-statement or suppression of facts on behalf of the Appellant. The decision of this Court in Uniworth Textiles (supra), has been relied upon by the Appellant. The same explains the situations in which Section 28 of the 1962 Act can be invoked. It had been held in the said decision that the extension of limitation for a period of five years can be done only in cases of deliberate default and not inadvertent non-payment. It was further held that the burden for proving mala fide conduct is on the revenue; and specific averments in that regard must find place in the show cause notice.

In the fact situation of the present case, the Appellant was issued a show cause notice mentioning that it had suppressed the DTA sales of cut flowers to evade payment of duty. Had the Appellant in good faith believed that no duty was payable upon the DTA sales of cut flowers, it would have sought prior approval of the Development Commissioner, which it failed to do. Even in the letter seeking ex-post facto approval, the Appellant claimed that they had not used any imported input such as fertilizer, plant growth Regulations, etc. in growing flowers sold in DTA, despite having imported green house equipment, raw materials like Live Rose Plants and consumables like planting materials and fertilizers. Therefore, it prima facie appeared that suppression by the Appellant was "wilful". The burden of proving to the contrary rested upon the Appellant, which the Appellant failed to discharge by failing to establish that the imported inputs were not used in the production of the cut flowers sold in DTA. In view thereof, the authorities below have rightly invoked Section 28 of the 1962 Act and allied provisions.

In light of the foregoing discussion and observations, we are of the view that CESTAT has rightly upheld the levy of customs duty.

This appeal, therefore, deserves to be dismissed. It is so ordered. There shall be no order as to costs. Pending applications, if any, shall stand disposed of.

IV

Remo Paul Altoe Vs. Union of India (UOI), 1977

Hon'ble Judges/Coram:A.C. Gupta and S. Murtaza Fazal Ali, JJ.

Relevant Section:

CUSTOMS ACT, 1962 - Section 135

Acts/Rules/Orders:

Customs Act, 1962 - Section 11, Section 11(2), Section 111, Section 112, Section 122,Section 124, Section 125, Section 126,Section 127, Section 135; Foreign Exchange Regulation Act, 1973 - Section 13, Section 13(1),

Equivalent Citation: AIR1977SC2255, [1978]48CompCas522(SC), 1977CriLJ1933, 1983(13)ELT1600(S.C.), (1977)4SCC437, [1978]1SCR719, 1977(9)UJ730MANU/SC/0372/1977

No. of pages in Original Judgement: 5

Case Note:

Customs - confiscation - Section 452 (1) of Criminal Procedure Code, 1973, Section 13 (1) of Foreign Exchange Regulation Act, 1973 and Section 135 of Customs Act, 1962 - an Order for disposal of any property under Section 452 (1) of Code is necessary where property remains to be disposed of by Court after inquiry or trial is over - foreign currency seized from appellant was not produced before Magistrate and was not in custody or control of Court when Order for confiscation was made - there was no necessity for Court to make an Order for disposal of any property - Order passed by

Magistrate clearly reveal that he was not aware what had happened to the goods - although foreign currency was seized from appellant's possession in respect of which an offence was committed but an Order under Section 452 (1) was unwarranted - such Order is likely to create complication if Customs authorities have made any Order which might be inconsistent with Order of Magistrate - held, Order of confiscation passed by Magistrate liable to be set aside.

Brief facts of the case:

This appeal is by special leave, from a Judgment of the Calcutta High Court, this Court in granting special leave limited the appeal to only one ground, whether the trial court had power to order confiscation of the goods found in appellant's possession while convicting him under Section 135 of the Customs Act.

The facts relevant for the purpose of the appeal are these. The; appellant is a foreigner who arrived at Calcutta by air from Bangkok on June 28, 1975. On a search of his room in the hotel where he was staying in Calcutta, the Customs authorities found in his possession 1701 U.S. dollars and 4400 Canadian dollars which they seized as smuggled goods. On September 23, 1975 an Assistant Collector of Customs filed a petition of complaint in the court of the Chief Metropolitan Magistrate, Calcutta, alleging, inter alia, that the appellant had brought in the foreign currency seized from his possession in violation of Section 13(1) of the Foreign Exchange Regulation Act, 1973 and was therefore liable to be convicted under Section 135 of the Customs Act, 1962. Section 13(1) of the Foreign Exchange Regulation Act, 1973 imposes restriction's on bringing or sending into India any gold or silver or any foreign exchange or any Indian currency. Section 67 of that Act provides:

Application of the Customs Act, 1962. The restrictions imposed by or under Section 13, Clause (a) of Sub-section (1) of Section 18 and Clause (a) of Sub-section (1) of Section 19 shall be deemed to have been imposed under Section 11 of the Customs Act, 1962 and all the provisions of that Act shall have effect accordingly.

Held,

The Customs Act thus provides that contraband goods "shall be liable to confiscation" and also lays down a detailed procedure for the confiscation of such goods. The appellant contends that the special provisions of the Customs Act regarding the confiscation of goods seized under that Act make the general law as to disposal of property contained in Section 452(1) of the

CrPC inapplicable in respect of such goods. According to the respondent Union of India, Customs authorities and the criminal court have concurrent jurisdictions in the matter. However, we do not find it necessary to answer the question in this appeal which, in our opinion, should succeed on a short point. An order for the disposal of any property under Section 452(1) of the CrPC is necessary where the property remains to be disposed of by the court after the inquiry or trial is over. In the present case it appears that the foreign currency seized from the appellant was not produced before the Magistrate and was not in the custody or control of the court when the order of confiscation was made. There was thus no necessity or occasion for the court to make an order for disposal of any property; the order of the magistrate that the goods involved in the case are confiscated "If not already confiscated" clearly shows that he was not aware what had happened to the goods which were in the control of the Customs authorities. It is true that the foreign currency seized from the appellant's possession was property in respect of which an offence was committed, but this fact alone did not call for an order under Section 452(1) in the circumstances of the case and that order passed, besides being unwarranted, is likely to create complications if in respect of the foreign currency a proceeding under the Customs Act is pending or the Customs authorities have made any order with which the magistrate's order is inconsistent. We therefore allow the appeal and set aside the order of confiscation passed by the magistrate and affirmed by the High Court.

Mr. Kohli, learned Counsel for the appellant, prays that the Customs authorities should be directed to return to appellant the currency seized from his possession. How the Customs authorities have dealt with the property, whether the appellant is entitled to have the foreign currency seized from his possession returned to him under any provision of the Customs Act, are not questions that arise for consideration in this appeal. The record of the case also does not contain any material upon which we could give any direction in the matter even if we wanted to. However, as this is an old case, we hope that the Customs authorities will take a decision in this matter according to law as early as possible.

V

Rasiklal Kantilal& Co. Vs. Board of Trustee of Port of Bombay and Ors., 2017

Hon'ble Judges/Coram: Justice Chelameswar and Abhay Manohar Sapre, JJ.

Relevant Section:

Customs Act, 1962 - Section 29; Indian Contract Act, 1872 - Section 158; Major Port Trusts Act, 1963 - Section 42(7)

Equivalent Citation: 2017(3)ABR44, AIR2017SC1283, 2017(2)BomCR823, 2017 (1) CCC 209 , 124(2017)CLT1074, 2017(II)CLR(SC)606, 2017(348)ELT3(S.C.), [2017]43GSTR402(SC), (2017)3MLJ844, 2017(3)SCALE195, (2017)11SCC1, 2017 (5) SCJ 126, MANU/SC/0220/2017

No. of pages in Original Judgement: 20

Case Note:

Commercial - Demurrage - Non-clearance of goods - Grant of remission of demand - Declining thereof - 1st Respondent demanded demurrage charges from Petitioner on ground that no remission could be granted prior to date of noting - 1st Respondent rejected request of Petitioner for grant of remission of demurrage - Aggrieved by order of 1st Respondent, Appellant filed petition - High Court dismissed petition - Hence, present appeal - Whether decision of 1st Respondent to decline grant of remission of entire demand towards demurrage on account of non-clearance of goods, was acceptable

Brief Facts of the case:

During the period in question, 78 shipments of zinc ingots and copper iron bars were imported by 5 different consignees from the original exporter; these consignments were landed at the Bombay Port. The consignees filed bills of entry for 37 out of the 78 consignments, but subsequently failed to lift the consignments and thus, they came to be stored at by the Port of Bombay. The consignments were shipped on "CAD Basis" i.e. cash against documents, in which the title to the goods would remain with the exporter till such a time the importer would retire the documents against payments. Facing a grave loss the original exporter, requested the Petitioner, if they were interested in purchasing the goods. The Petitioner and the original consignees were no where related, and the Petitioner was a third party to the sales. On 23.03.1992, the Petitioner through his agent applied to the Customs Authorities to have the Bills of Entry substituted in their name for the 37 consignments for which the original consignees had filed Bills of Entry, and also applied to file Bills of Entry for the remaining 41 consignments lying unclaimed. The formal agreement between the original exporter and the Petitioner was entered subsequently, in April of 1992.

Held,

Application of sale proceeds (1) The proceeds of every sale Under Section 61 or Section 62 shall be applied in the following order-

(a) in payment of the expenses of the sale;

(b) in payment, according to their respective priorities, of the liens and claims excepted in Sub-section (2) of Section 59 from the priority of the lien of the Board;

(c) in payment of the rates and expenses of landing, removing, storing or warehousing the same, and of all other charges due to the Board in respect thereof including demurrage (other than penal demurrage) payable in respect of such goods for a period of four months from the date of landing.

(d) in payment of any penalty or fine due to Central Government under any law for the time being in force relating to customs;(e) in payment of any other sum due to the Board.

(2) The surplus, if any, shall be paid to the importer, owner or consignee of the goods or to his agent, on an application made by him in this behalf within six months from the date of the sale of the goods.

(3) Where no application has been made under Sub-section (2), the surplus shall be applied by the Board for the purposes of this Act.Board of Trustees of the Port of **Bombay and Ors. v. Sriyanesh Knitters**MANU/SC/0431/1999 : (1999) 7 SCC 359.

"16. There is another aspect which is relevant. Section 171 of the Contract Act only enables the retention of goods as security. On the other hand in respect of current dues in respect of existing goods in their possession the Board not only has a lien Under Section 59 of the MPT Act but it also has the power to sell the said goods and realise its dues by virtue of Section 61 of the MPT Act. The procedure for exercising this power of sale of the goods in respect of which the Board has lien is contained in the said section. **Before selling the goods no order of any court or other judicial authority is required.** On the other hand the general lien contemplated by Section 171 of the Contract Act only enables the retention of the bailed goods as a security. Their retention does not give any power to sell the goods, unlike the power contained in Section 61 of the MPT Act. If payment is not made by the consignee to the wharfinger, in a case where Section 171 of the Contract Act applies, the wharfinger can only retain the goods bailed as security and will have to take recourse to other proceedings in accordance with law for securing an order which would then enable the goods to be sold for realisation of the amounts due to it. It may in this connection, be necessary for the wharfinger to file a suit for the recovery of the amount due to it and Section 131 of the MPT Act clearly provides that such a remedy of filing a suit is available to the Board."It is not very clear from the record whether these guidelines were issued by the Government of India or guidelines framed by the 1st Respondent. In the written submissions, the Appellant describes the guidelines framed by the Government of India whereas under the judgment under appeal at para 24, it appears that the Appellant's case before the High Court was that they were guidelines framed by the 1st Respondent.He would submit that the guidelines framed by the BPT itself provides for remission asked for by the Petitioners when the detention of the goods by the Custom was for bonafide operation of ITC formalities." Per contra the case of the 1st Respondent before the High Court regarding the guidelines appears to beremission is granted on ex-gratia basis, that too, by exercising discretion on the basis of guidelines issued by the Union of India and adopted by resolution passed by Respondent No. 1 along with Custom Department."

The High Court did not record any categorical finding in this regard except stating. In exercise of statutory powers Under Section 101 of the Major Port

Trust Act guidelines for remission of demurrage charges are framed."

See International Airports Authority of India v. Grand Slam International MANU/SC/0653/1995 : (1995) 3 SCC 151

The full factual background as to how it all happened is not relevant for our purpose.

VI

O. Konavalov Vs. Commander, Coast Guard Region and Ors., 2006

Hon'ble Judges/Coram: H.K. Sema and A.R. Lakshmanan, JJ.

Relevant Section:

Customs Act, 1962 - Section 110, Section 112(a), Section 115, Section 115(2), Section 126, Section 30

Equivalent Citation: 2006(4)ALT1(SC), 2006(2)CTC672, 2006(132)ECR379(SC), 2006(197)ELT3(S.C.), JT2006(3)SC567, 2006(3)SCALE398, (2006)4SCC620, MANU/SC/1550/2006

No. of pages in Original Judgement: 14

Case Note:

Customs - Wages - Maritime lien - Appellant filed an application to pay wages from the sale proceeds of cargo or a direction for sale of ship and pay wages as first charge - Respondent stated that since the vessel was confiscated there was no question of first charge - Whether the crew was entitled to wages - Held, crewmen by virtue of them being crewmen have a lien on the vessel and were entitled to claim such wages that were due to them - Rationale being wage lien arises from services rendered to the ship members of ship from the date of engagement till deportation - Crew were entitled to wages - Section 115 of the Customs Act, 1962 would not disentitle the crew of the lien for recovery of wages as it was an established practice in the lawof seas - Seamen entitled to full wages - Appeals allowed

Brief Factsof the case:

A foreign vessel with foreign crewmen was spotted by the customs department in Indian territorial waters. Cargo was treated as smuggled goods and confiscation of ship ensued owing to confiscation of goods. Subsequently, an interim order was passed. Later, the ship was sold. The appellant filed an application claiming wages out of the sale of the ship. The Single Judge of the High Court allowed the application, allowing payment of wages and deportation of crew on government expenses. On appeal, the Division Bench of the High Court held that since confiscation of goods were proceedings in rem, consequent upon the confiscation of the ship, the property in the ship, including all interests attached to the ship got forfeited and did not admit of any exception. Hence, the present appeal.

Held,

This Court in various judgments beginning from R.C.Cooper's case and Maneka Gandhi's case etc. have laid down that deprivation of rights is subject to judicial review. The State action is restrained by principles of reasonableness, justice and fair play. The principles enshrined in Article 21 are equally applicable to a foreigner as it is to a citizen. The confiscation by the Government of the vessel cannot extinguish the pre- existing rights of the crew men. India has become a signatory to various International Conventions honouring the social, political, civil, economic rights of human beings. The Directive Principles of State Policy has also become fundamental right and justifiable.

The Merchant Shipping Act, 1958 has laid down exhaustive provisions for seamen's wages. The Act itself recognizes that recovery of wages shall not be subject to attachment. Section 445 of the Act provides that payment of wages of Seamen can be made by sale of ship. In the Companies Act, under Section 529(a) an overriding effect has been given and it has been provided that in winding up proceedings the worker's dues have priority over other claims. The Madras High Court has failed to appreciate that India has travelled very far from 1950 and that the Courts have given way to a dynamic constructive approach in the aspect of social justice while referring to International Conventions etc.

We, therefore, unhesitant hold that all the seamen who were on board the vessel Kobe Queen I also known as Gloria Kopp are entitled to their full wages and perks. We, therefore, direct the Commander Coast Guard

Region (East), Fort St. George, Chennai - 600 009 and the other respondents including the Customs Department and the concerned Department of the Government of India to pay the wages forthwith to all the crew members who were on board in the vessel Kobe Queen I also known as Gloria Kopp at any rate not later than three months from the date of this judgment through the Consulate of the country concerned.

We place on record our deep appreciation for the valuable assistance rendered by senior counsel Mr. Venkataramani and Mr. Ravi P. Mehrotra who made our job easier. In the result, the order impugned in these appeals passed by the Division Bench of the Madras High Court is set aside and the appeals stand allowed. However, we order no costs.

VII

International Airports Authority of India and Ors. Vs. Grand Slam International and Ors., 1995

Hon'ble Judges/Coram: R.M. Sahai, S.P. Bharucha and N.G. Venkatachala, JJ.

Relevant Section:

CUSTOMS ACT, 1962 - Section 45

Equivalent Citation: 58(1995)DLT530(SC), 1995(50)ECC4, 1995(57)ECR209(SC), 1995(77)ELT753(S.C.), JT1995(2)SC452, 1995(1)SCALE859, (1995)3SCC151, [1995]2SCR149, MANU/SC/0653/1995

No. of pages in Original Judgement: 23

Case Note:

Customs - Detention Certificate--Demurrage--Adjudication Proceedings--Custodian--Delayed clearance-- Jurisdiction--Indian Airports Authority Act, 1971-- Cust. Act, 1962 (S. 45) does not contain any provision that the Custodian of goods is not entitled to recover charges for the period (taken up in adjudication proceedings and caused delay in clearance of imported goods) covered by the Detention Certificate issued by the Customs Authorities--Such direction could be issued under S. 35 of the IAA Act, 1971 for which Customs do not have jurisdiction--Cus. Act 1962, S. 45.

Brief Facts of the case:

The Appellants, custodians of imported goods, demanded demurrage from the Assessees for the period during which adjudication proceedings were pending before the Customs Authorities. The Department issued Detention Certificates u/s. 45, Customs Act, 1962 asking the Appellants not to charge demurrage for the period of pendency of proceedings. But the Appellants ignored the same. On writ petitions filed by the Assessees, the High Court held that the Appellants being custodians of the Customs Department, were bound by the Detention Certificates and no demurrages could be charged for the periods shown in the certificates.

Demurrage--Delayed Clearance--Detention Certificate--Custodian--Adjudication Proceedings--Section 45 Customs Act does not state that the custodians of the imported goods (in this case, the IAAI and CWC) shall not be entitled to recover charges from the importer for such period as the Customs Authorities direct. That the custodian may not allow the importer to remove the goods without the permission of the proper officer of the Customs Deptt. does not imply that the importer will not be charged for the space occupied by his goods till clearance. If the intention is not to levy demurrage charges for the periods covered by the Detention Certificates, the Central Government could issue directions u/s. 35 of the IAA Act, 1971 after giving the IAAI an opportunity of expressing its views. ...."Section 45 provides that all imported goods imported in a Customs area must remain in the custody of the person who has been approved by the Collector of Customs until they are cleared and such person is obliged not to permit them to be removed from the Customs area or otherwise dealt with except under and in accordance with the permission of the Customs officer. Section 45 does not state that such person shall not be entitled to recover charges from the importer for such period as the Customs authorities direct."

Held,

The Central Warehousing Corporation established under the provisions of the Warehousing Corporation Act, 1962 is a creature of statute as is the IAAI under the International Airports Authority Act, 1971. The entitlement of the CWC to recover demurrages for the goods of which it becomes the custodian under the provisions of the Act cannot be different from that of the IAAI, as indicated in the earlier judgment. If that be so, what I have said in the aforesaid appeals of the IAAI would equally apply to the CWC also. The High Court having directed the Customs authorities to issue detention certificates in respect of the goods of which the CWC was the owner has relieved the importer respondent-1 in the appeal from his liability to pay demurrage charges. Because of the view I have taken in my judgment in the earlier appeals it has to be held that the High Court's direction relieving respondent-1 from his liability to pay demurrage charges cannot be sustained.

In the result, Civil Appeal Nos. 798 of 1992, 3971 of 1992 and 4227 of 1992 are allowed. The judgments of the High Court under appeals are set aside. The Writ Petitions filed by respondent-1 in each of the cases before the High Court are dismissed. In the facts of the present appeals, there shall be no order as to costs.

For reasons given by us in our separate judgments (R.M. Sahai, J. for dismissal of the appeals whereas S.P. Bharucha and N.G. Venkatachala, JJ. for allowing the appeals) the appeals succeed and are allowed. The orders passed by the High Court are set aside. And the Writ Petition shall stand dismissed. But in the circumstances of the case, there shall be no order as to costs.

VIII

Shipping Corporation of India Ltd. and Ors. vs. C. L. Jain Woolen Mills and Ors., 2001

Hon'ble Judges/Coram: G.B. Pattanaik, S.N. Phukan and B.N. Agrawal, JJ.

Relevant Section:

CUSTOMS ACT, 1962 - Section 45

Equivalent Citation: AIR2001SC1806, 2001(3)BLJ671, 2001(75)ECC225, 2001(96)ECR625(SC), 2001(129)ELT561(S.C.), JT2001(4)SC507, (2001)3MLJ51(SC), 2001(3)SCALE279, (2001)5SCC345, [2001]2SCR1080, MANU/SC/0244/2001

No. of pages in Original Judgement: 8

Case Note:

Held: Demurrage Charges - Container Charges--Imported goods not released--Detained By Customs--Demurrage charges are levied and collected by the carrier/custodian of the goods for the space the goods occupy and for the period the goods remain stored, beyond the prescribed free period, on account of non-clearance by customs/owner of the goods. The carrier-custodian has the right to claim and collect demurrage charges in respect of the goods not released, under the terms and conditions of the contract between the importer and the carrier (see S. 170 of the Contract Act, and Clauses 14 and 18 of the Bills of Lading Act). This right is not nullified by the issue of a Detention Certificate by the customs authorities. The Customs Act does not empower the customs authorities to direct the carrier/custodian not to charge the demurrage charges--ratio of Supreme Court judgment in the case of Grand Slant International. Cus. Act: S. 45(2). "............the very terms of the contract and the provisions of the Bills of Lading, unequivocally conferred power on the appellant to retain the goods, until the dues are paid. Such rights accruing in favour of the appellant cannot be nullified by issuance of a certificate of detention by the customs authorities unless for such issuance of detention certificate any provisions of the Customs Act authorises. We had not been shown any provisions of the Customs Act, which would enable the customs authorities to compel the carrier, not to charge demurrage charges, the moment a detention certificate is issued. It may be undoubtedly true that the customs authorities might have bona fide initiated the proceedings for confiscation of the goods which however, ultimately turned out to be unsuccessful and the Court held the same to be illegal. But that by itself, would not clothe the customs authorities with the power to direct the carrier who continues to retain a lien over the imported goods, so long as his dues are not paid, not to charge any demurrage charges nor the so-called issuance of detention certificate would also prohibit the carrier from raising any demand towards demurrage charges, for the occupation of the imported goods of the space, which the proprietor of the space is entitled to charge from the importer. The importer also will not be entitled to remove his goods from the premises unless customs clearance is given. But that would not mean that demurrage charges could not be levied on importer for the space his goods have occupied, since the contract between the importer and the proprietor of the space is in no way altered because of the orders issued by the customs authorities. ....the expression "otherwise dealt with" used in Section 45(2)(b), and therefore, the proprietor of the space would be bound not to charge any demurrage charges. We are unable to accept this contention inasmuch as the expression "otherwise dealt with" used in Section 45(2)(b), in the context in which it has been used, cannot be construed to mean, it authorises the customs officer to issue a detention certificate in respect of the imported goods, which would absolve the importer from paying the demurrage charges and which would prevent the proprietor of the space from levying any demurrage charges. Having scrutinized the provisions of the Customs Act, we are unable to find out any provision which can be remotely construed to have conferred power on the customs authorities to prevent the proprietor of the space from levying the demurrage charges and, thereby absolving the importer of the goods from payment of the same.

Brief Facts of the case:

In this batch of appeals, a common question of law having arisen, they were heard together and are being disposed of by this common judgment. The question for consideration is whether the appellant, who under the terms of the contract between him and the owner of the goods, having a lien over the goods, until the dues are paid can be forced to release the goods, without charging any demurrage, merely because the customs authorities issued a detention order for a specified period? We would discuss the question in relation to the facts in the case between the Shipping Corporation of India vs. C.L. Jain Woolen Mills. The respondent C.L. Jain Woolen Mills, imported the consignment of polyester filament yarn from Korea to India. The port of load was Bussan in Korea and the port of discharge was Bombay in India, but the place of delivery of goods was ICD, Delhi. The goods thus being brought to the port of Bombay were discharged but there had been no customs clearance at Bombay and the sealed container was transhipped to ICD, Delhi, where it remained with the Container Corporation of India. The Shipping Corporation of India is engaged in the business of carriage of goods. On the terms and conditions contained in the Bill of Lading, in respect of the goods consigned to it, the corporation claims that the goods cannot be released unless demurrage charges are paid. After the goods arrived in Delhi and remained in the custody of the appellant, the customs authorities being of the opinion that import of polyester filament yarn weighing 5.376 kgs. was unauthorised and directed confiscation of the same valued at Rs.11.5 lakhs under Section 111(d) of the Customs Act, 1962. The said customs authorities however permitted the owner to redeem the goods on payment of Rs. 7 lakhs. That apart, a penalty of Rs. 1 lakh was also levied under Section 112(a) of the Customs Act. The owner of the goods assailed the order before the Customs, Excise & Gold (Control) Appellate Tribunal [for short CEGAT]. The tribunal instead of deciding the objections raised by the owner to the validity of the order of the Additional Collector of Customs, ordered that the advance licence and DEEC Book be amended and adjourned the appeal for a period of three months. The owner, therefore, approached the Delhi High Court by filing a writ petition, which was registered as Writ Petition No. 1604/91, praying quashing of the order of the customs authorities, confiscating the goods and imposing the penalty and that of the Import Trade Control Authority enhancing the export obligation from 14,497.5 kgs. to 22,330 kgs. of polyester fabric. It was the contention of the owner before the High Court that in accordance with the export policy and the "Duty Exemption Scheme", raw materials could be cleared for home consumption without payment of import duty. To avail of the facility, the importer is required to apply for grant of licence called the 'Advance Licence' and on the basis of the same, raw materials could be imported without payment of any duty. According to the owner, under the licence, thus issued by the Controller of Imports and Exports, entitling import of raw materials without payment of duty, the customs authorities committed error in proceeding with the confiscation proceedings and ordering confiscation as well as levying penalty. The customs authorities as well as the Controller of Imports and Exports had been arrayed as party respondents in the writ petition. Both of them as well as Union of India resisted the claim of the owner, who had imported the goods in question. The High Court disposed of the writ petition by judgment dated 9th September, 1994, quashing the order of the Additional Collector of Customs dated 10th August, 1990 as well as the order of the Customs Excise and Gold (Control) Appellate Tribunal dated 21st March, 1991 and directed the Collector of Customs to release the goods forthwith. The High Court also further held that since the action of the custom authorities is illegal, the goods in question will have to be released to the owner without payment of any detention or demurrage charges by the owner. Needless to mention, the Shipping Corporation of India, the appellant in the present appeal, who was the carrier and who under the Bills of Lading had a lien over the goods, until the dues are paid had not been made a party to the aforesaid writ petition. At this stage it may also be noticed that during pendency of the writ petition in the High Court, an interim order had been passed, entitling the owner to take release of the goods on payment of Rs. 5 lakhs to customs authorities and a bank guarantee of Rs. 5 lakhs but the owner had not taken advantage of the said interim order and the goods continued to remain in the custody of the present appellant and demurrage charges went on accruing. The order of Delhi High Court was assailed in this Court by filing a Special Leave Petition by the Customs Authorities but that Special Leave Petition however stood dismissed on 13.11.95 in SLP No. 5671/95. The owner of the goods having failed in his attempt to get the goods released, notwithstanding the orders of the High Court in CWP No. 1604/91, filed an application for initiating a contempt proceeding, which was registered as CCP No. 120/95. The High Court however came to hold that the authorities cannot be held to be guilty of disobeying the orders of the Court and accordingly, dismissed the contempt petition. While dismissing the contempt petition, the learned Judge, granted liberty to the owner to move the Division Bench of the High Court for appropriate directions regarding payment of demurrage/detention charges. Pursuant to the aforesaid observations in the contempt proceedings, an application being filed by the owner, the same was registered as CM 4829/96. That application was disposed of by the Division Bench of Delhi High Court by order dated 18th January, 1999. The Division Bench, while disposing of the petition, came to hold that the entitlement of the carrier of the goods to charge demurrage charges and if so, whether the customs authorities would be liable to pay the same or not is not required to be answered and is a matter, which should be sorted out between those two corporations and the customs authorities. But so far as the owner of the goods are concerned, he having been absolved of any liability to pay the demurrage charges by virtue of the judgment of Delhi High Court dated 9.9.94 in CWP No. 1604/91, he would be entitled to get the goods released without payment of the detention and demurrage charges. The High Court, therefore called upon the customs department as well as the two corporations, who are the carriers to sort out the matter within a specified period and further held that if any detention or demurrages charges are payable, the same shall be paid by the customs department within three weeks. It further directed the carrier of the goods, including the appellant to released the goods after the customs department pays the detention/demurrage charges. Notwithstanding the aforesaid order, the goods not being released, when a fresh contempt petition was filed, registered as CCP No. 89/99, the High Court issued notice on 25.2.99, calling upon the alleged contemnor to file their reply by 11th March, 1999. Against the initiation of the aforesaid contempt proceeding, the Shipping Corporation of India filed SLP No. 3391/99. The order dated 18.1.99 was also assailed by the Shipping Corporation, which was registered as SLP No. 5001/ 99. The container Corporation of India filed a special leave petition on identical circumstances and raising identical question, which is SLP No. 9021/99. The Union of India also assails the order dated 18.1.99 by filing Special Leave Petition No. 3063/2001 along with the application for condonation of delay. This batch of cases were listed before a Bench of two learned Judges on 11th February, 2001 and after hearing the matters for sometime, the Bench felt that there appears to be some inconsistency between the decision of this Court in ***Union of India vs. Sanjeev Woolen***

Mills MANU/SC/0378/1998 : **1998(100)ELT323(SC)** and the ***Grand Slam International's case*** MANU/SC/0653/1995 : ***1995ECR209(SC)*** : ***1995ECR209(SC)*** and as such observed that the cases should be placed before a Three Judge Bench and that is how, this batch of cases are before this three Judge Bench. When these appeals by grant of special leave were placed before the Three Judge Bench on 1st March, 2001, we had directed the goods be released to the owner without any conditions but such release will be subject to the ultimate decision in these appeals.

Held,

Before examining the correctness of the rival submissions, one thing is crystal clear that the relationship between the importer and the carrier of goods in whose favour the Bill of lading has been consigned and who has stored the goods in his custody, the relationship is governed by the contract between the parties. Section 170 of the Indian Contract Act engraft the principle of Bailee's lien, namely if somebody has received the articles on being delivered to him and is required to store the same until cleared for which he might have borne the expenses, he has a right to detain it until his dues are paid. But it is not necessary in the case in hand to examine the common law principle and the bailee's lien inasmuch as the very terms of the contract and the provisions of the Bills of Lading,, unequivocally conferred power on the appellant to retain the goods, until the dues are paid. Such rights accruing in favour of the appellant cannot be nullified by issuance of a certificate of detention by the customs authorities unless for such issuance of detention certificate any provisions of the Customs Act authorities. We have not been shown any provisions of the Customs Act, which would enable the customs authorities to compel the carrier, not to charge demurrage charges, the moment a detention certificate is issued. It may be undoubtedly true that the customs authorities might have bona fide initiated the proceedings for confiscation of the goods which however, ultimately turned out to be unsuccessful and the Court held the same to be illegal. But that by itself, would not clothe the customs authorities with the power to direct the carrier who continues to retain a lien over the imported goods, so long as his dues are not paid, not to change any demurrage charges not the so-called issuance of detention certificate would also prohibit the carrier from raising any demand towards demurrage charges, for the occupation of the imported goods of the space, which the proprietor of the space is entitled to charge from the importer. The importer also will not be entitled to remove his goods from the premises unless customs clearance is given. But that would not mean that demurrage charges could not be levied on importer for the space his goods have occupied, since the contract between the importer and the proprietor of the space is in no way altered because of the orders issued by the customs authorities. The learned Additional Solicitor General, vehemently argued and pressed sub-section 2(b) of Section 45 in support of his contention that the imported goods have to be dealt with in accordance with the permission in writing of the proper officer of the customs department and in exercise of such power when customs authorities initiate adjudication proceeding and ultimately confiscate and levy penalty, when such order is struck down and a detention certificate is issued, the said issuance of detention certificate would come within the expression "otherwise dealt with" used in Section 45(2)(b), and therefore, the proprietor of the space would be bound not to charge any demurrage charges. We are unable to accept this contention inasmuch as the expression "otherwise dealt with" used in Section 45(2)(b), in the context in which it has been used, cannot be construed to mean, it authorises the customs officer to issue a detention certificate in respect of the imported goods, which would absolve the importer from paying the demurrage charges and which would prevent the proprietor of the space from levying any demurrage charges. Having scrutinized the provisions of the Customs Act, we are unable to find out any provision which can be remotely construed to have conferred power on the customs authorities to prevent the proprietor of the space from levying the demurrage charges and, thereby absolving the importer of the goods from payment of the same. In fact the majority decision in ***Grand Slam International's case*** **MANU/SC/0653/1995** ***: 1995ECR209(SC) : 1995ECR209(SC)*** , clearly comes to the aforesaid conclusion with which we respectfully agree.

10. We have also examined the decision of this Court in ***Union of India vs. Sanjeev Woolen Mills*** MANU/SC/0378/1998 ***: 1998(100)ELT323(SC)*** and we do not find any apparent inconsistency between the decision of this Court in ***Grand Slam*** and that of the ***Sanjeev Woolen Mills.*** In Sanjeev Woolen Mills, the imported goods were synthetic waste (soft quality), though the customs authorities detained the same, being of the opinion that they were prime fibre of higher value and not soft waste. On account of non-release, the imported goods incurred heavy demurrage charges but the customs authorities themselves gave an undertaking before the High Court that in the event the goods are found to be synthetic waste, then the Revenue itself would bear the entire demurrage and container charges. Further the Chief

Commissioner of Customs, later had ordered unconditional release of goods and yet the goods had not been released. It is under these circumstances and in view of the specific undertaking given by the customs authorities, this Court held that from the date of detention of the goods till the customs authorities intimated the importer, the importer would not be required to pay the demurrage charges. But in that case even subsequent to the orders of the customs authorities on a suit being filed by one of the partners of the importer-firm, an order of injunction was issued and, therefore it was held that for that period, the importer would be liable for paying the demurrage and container charges. The judgment of this Court in ***Sanjeev Woolen Mills***, therefore, was in relation to the peculiar facts and circumstances of the case and the Court had clearly observed that the order in question is meant to do justice to the importer, looking to the totality of the circumstances and the conduct of customs authorities. Thus, we see no inconsistency between the ratio in ***Sanjeev Wollen Mills*** and the Judgment of this Court in ***Grand Slam***. That apart, the judgment in ***Grind Slam*** was a three judge bench judgment. In the case in hand, as has already been stated earlier, the earlier judgment of Delhi High Court dated 9.9.94 in C.W.P. No. 1604/91, has become final, which entitles the importer to get the goods released without payment of the detention and demurrage charges. In the contextual facts, notwithstanding the judgment of the High Court, the goods not having been released, the impugned order and direction dated 18.1.99, cannot be held to be infirm in any manner. In the absence of any provision in the Customs Act, entitling the customs officer to prohibit the owner of the space, where the imported goods have been stored from levying the demurrage charges, levy of demurrage charges for non-release of the goods is in accordance with the terms and conditions of the contract and as such would be a valid levy. The conclusion of the High Court to the effect that the detention of the goods by the customs authorities was illegal and such illegal detention prevented the importer from releasing the goods, the customs authorities would be bound to bear the demurrage charges in the absence of any provision in the Customs Act, absolving the customs authorities from that liability. Section 45(2)(b) of the Customs Act cannot be construed to have clothed the customs authorities with the necessary powers, so as to absolve them of the liability of paying the demurrage charges. In the aforesaid premises, we see no infirmity with the directions given by the Delhi High Court on 18.1.99. The goods in question, having already been directed to be released, without the payment of the demurrage charges, the importer must have got the goods released. Having regard to the fact situation of the present case, it would be meet and paper for us to direct the Shipping Corporation and Container Corporation, if an application is filed by the customs authorities to waive the demurrage charges. The appeal is disposed of accordingly.

IX

Northern Plastic Limited Vs. Collector of Customs & Central Excise, 1998

Hon'ble Judges/Coram: S.C. Agrawal and G.T. Nanavati, JJ.

Relevant Section:

Customs Act, 1962 - SECTION 11(m); SECTION 11(d)

Equivalent Citation: 1998VAD(SC)261, AIR1998SC2371, 1998(62)ECC2, 1998(77)ECR666(SC), 1998(101)ELT549(S.C.), JT1998(4)SC565, 1998(4)SCALE105, (1998)6SCC443, [1998]3SCR611, MANU/SC/0418/1998

No. of pages in Original Judgement: 7

Case Note:

Facts: Three main issues are involved in the present case, in which the Tribunal's order of fine in lieu of confiscation of imported goods as well as imposition of penalty is under challenge. The first issue is that of classification. The appellants classified the "Cinematographic Colour Films (Unexposed) Positive" imported by them under CTA: SH. 3702.41 for customs duty purposes and under CETA: SH. 3702.20 for CVD purposes, whereas the customs authorities held that the goods were actually "jumbo rolls" of "Photographic Colour Films (Unexposed) Positive" and had been mis-declared. The second issue is the charge of attempting to evade duty by wrongly describing the goods in order to avail of exemptions to which the appellants' goods were not entitled. The third issue is that of illegal import, where the appellants, a registered small scale unit, have been held not to be "actual users (industrial)" in terms of the Industries (D & R) Act read with the Factories Act and, therefore, not entitled to import the impugned goods under OGL.

Brief Facts of the case:

The appellant in both these appeals is Northern Plastics Limited. Civil Appeal No. 4196 of 1989 is filed against the order of remand dated 14.8.89 passed by the Customs, Excise and Gold (Control) Appellate Tribunal (hereinafter referred to as the 'CEGAT') in Customs Appeal No. 2092/89-C. Civil Appeal No. 3325 of 1990 is filed against the order dated 20.4.90 passed by the CEGAT in Customs Appeal No. 2720/89-C, which appeal was against the order of the Collector passed after the remand.

In January 1989 the appellant imported 59 jumbo rolls of Photographic Colour Films (Unexposed) Positive. On or about 11.1.89 it produced before the Deputy Collector of Customs, Kandla Port the documents required for clearance of the said goods wherein the goods were described as "Cinematographic Colour Films (Unexposed) Positive" falling under Customs Tariff Heading 3702.41 and the Central Excise Tariff Item 3702.20 and entitled to exemption of customs duty under Notification No. 52/86 read with Notification No. 157/88-Customs and of countervailing duty under Notification No. 50/88-C.Ex. Clearance of the goods was sought under OGL, the imported goods being Item No. 186 (1) of Part I of List 8 of Appendix 6 of AM 85-88.

Held,

What has been held by CEGAT is that the appellant required an industrial licence issued under the IDR Act as slitting and cutting of jumbo rolls, was a controlled/scheduled industry under that Act. Under that Act it was necessary for a new industrial undertaking to obtain a licence if it was an undertaking pertaining to a scheduled industry carried on in a factory. CEGAT relying upon these provisions of IDR Act and the definition of factory as contained in Factories Act held that the appellant's undertaking being a new undertaking was required to obtain a licence as it was pertaining to a scheduled industry carried on in its factory. It was, however, contended by Mr. Dave, learned counsel for the appellant that CEGAT committed a grave error of law in relying upon the definition of 'factory' as contained in the Factories Act even though it was required to go by the definition of factory as contained in the IDR Act. He rightly submitted that as the IDR Act itself contains definition of word "factory" that definition should have been considered instead of the definition given in the Factories Act. The IDR Act defines factory to mean "any premises, including precincts thereof, in any part of which a manufacturing process is carried on or is ordinarily so carried on- (i) with the aid of power, provided that fifty or more workers are working or were working thereon on any day of the preceding twelve months; or (ii)....". It also defines industrial undertaking to mean any undertaking pertaining to a scheduled industry carried on in one or more factories by any person. Thus, the position under the IDR Act was that unless the scheduled industry was carried on in a factory as defined by the IDR Act, it was not required to take out a licence even though it was an undertaking pertaining to a scheduled industry. This aspect has been totally overlooked by CEGAT. Even the guidelines issued by the Government of India, Ministry of Industry for the benefit of the industries stated that no industrial licence was necessary if the industrial undertaking was not carried on in a factory as defined by the IDR Act. It was the case of the appellant, and it had produced material in support of it, that in its factory not more than twelve workers were ever employed. This fact was not disputed by the Customs authorities. It thus becomes clear that the appellant's industrial undertaking, though engaged in the industrial activity pertaining to the scheduled industry, was not carrying on such industry in a factory as defined by the Act. It was, therefore, not necessary for it to obtain a licence under the IDR Act. It did have a certificate of registration issued by the Director of Industries, Uttar Pradesh. Even the definition of 'actual user (industrial)' which we have quoted above makes it clear that licence under the IDR Act was required if the provision of the IDR Act in that behalf was applicable. As pointed out earlier, for the purpose of answering the definition of 'actual user (industrial)' it was not necessary for the appellant to obtain a licence under the IDR Act. It was sufficient, for the appellant to be called an actual user (industrial), to have a certificate of registration issued by the competent authority. The CEGAT was, therefore, in error in holding that importation of 59 jumbo rolls of Cinematographic Films by the appellant was unlawful and, therefore, liable to confiscation.

Therefore, neither on the ground of misdeclaration nor on the ground of import being unauthorized or illegal, the goods imported by the appellant were liable to confiscation. We, therefore, allow these appeal, set aside the order of confiscation and also the order levying fine of Rs. 5 lakhs in lieu of confiscation. We also set aside the order of penalty imposed upon the appellant. In view of the facts and circumstances of the cases, the parties shall bear their own cost.

X

Associated Cement Companies Ltd. and Ors. vs.Commissioner of Customs, 2001

Hon'ble Judges/Coram: B.N. Kirpal, Doraiswamy Raju and K.G. Balakrishnan, JJ.

Relevant Section:

Customs Act, 1962 - Section 2(22)

Equivalent Citation: AIR2001SC862, 2001(74)ECC1, 2001(95)ECR6(SC), 2001(128)ELT21(S.C.), JT2001(2)SC141, 2001(1)SCALE436, (2001)4SCC593, [2001]1SCR608, [2001]124STC59(SC), MANU/SC/0051/2001

No. of pages in Original Judgement: 17

Case Note:

Facts: The appellants had entered into various agreements/contracts with their foreign collaborators/consultants for supply of technical know-how, etc. In terms of the said agreements, the appellants received, through couriers, designs, drawings, plans, etc., which in each case were cleared, on the nominal declared value of one dollar, free of duty. Later, after investigations into these imports, issue of show cause notices and receipt of appellants' replies, the Commissioner, by the impugned order, held that the designs, drawings, plans, etc. relating to industrial technology or machinery were "goods", that customs duty was payable on the transaction value of these items at the time of their import, confirmed demand, and imposed penalty. The Commissioner's order was upheld by the Appellate Tribunal. Hence, these appeals before the Apex Court.

Brief facts of the case:

These appeals have been filed against the common order dated 15th November, 1999 of the Customs, Excise and Gold (Control) Appellate Tribunal which, while confirming the order of the Commissioner of Customs held that drawings, designs etc. relating to machinery or industrial technology were goods which were leviable to duty of customs on their transaction value at the time of their import.

As principal arguments on behalf of the appellants were addressed in the case of M/s Hotel Leela Ventures Limited by Mr. Ashok H. Desai, learned senior counsel, for the sake of convenience we will refer to the relevant facts in that case in greater detail.

Leela Ventures are engaged in the business of setting up, operating and maintaining Hotels and Resorts. For designing the Hotels and Resorts, it engaged a foreign company M/s Wimberly Allison Tong & Goo, USA ("WAT" for short) for providing architectural services including design development drawings. Leela Ventures had entered into four agreements with the said foreign company in respect of four different ventures in India. Apart from preparing the designs and drawings the scope of work under the said agreements included site visits and on site consultations with architects.

Held,

In the show cause notice which was issued it was proposed to regard the drawings which had come through the courier at DM 60,000 equivalent to Rs. 11,03,800/- as being subject to levy of duty. In the show cause notice it was stated that these technical drawings were supplied by the German company and being goods imported through courier services were classifiable under heading No. 98.03 and duty and penalty was payable in respect thereof.

Unlike other cases, we find that these drawings in respect of which customs duty had been levied were not something which had originated from Germany. These drawings were prepared by the Indian company of which the German company was a shareholder. These drawings were no doubt sent to Germany for approval but the agreement between the parties does not show that the payment of DM 60,000 was directly relatable or attributable to the approval and despatch of the said drawings to India. Under the agreements between the parties apart from the licence fee payable by the Indian company, for the use of the name of the German company and engineering fee, money was payable in terms of the agreement. As we have already observed there is nothing to show that this amount of DM 60,000 was relatable only to the approval of the said designs and drawings.

Be that as it may the value of these drawings which belong to the Indian company were merely approved by the German company could only be nominal and under no circumstances the said value could be regarded as DM 60,000. The nominal value disclosed by the courier, on the facts and circumstances of this case, could not, therefore, be said to be incorrect. The order passed against the appellant levying the customs duty and penalty is, therefore, to be set aside. Ordered accordingly.

Conclusion: As a result of the aforesaid discussion, Civil Appeal No. 1493 of 2000 of M/s H & K Rolling Mill Engineers Pvt. Ltd. and Civil Appeal No. 3632 of 2000 of M/s Videocon VCR Ltd. are allowed and the orders of the Commissioner and Customs, Excise-Gold (control) Appellate Tribunal in their cases are set aside. The other appeals are dismissed but in the case of Leela Ventures, out of the total contract value, the Commissioner will determine the transaction value of the drawings, designs, etc. imported through the courier and then impose the levy thereon. There will be no order as to costs.

XI

Department of Customs Vs. Sharad Gandhi, 2019

Hon'ble Judges/Coram: Ashok Bhushan and K.M. Joseph, JJ.

Relevant Section:

Customs Act, 1962 - Section 135; Section 132; Antiquities And Art Treasures Act 1972 - Section 3

Equivalent Citation: 258(2019)DLT81, 2019(366)ELT10(S.C.), 2019(4)SCALE312, (2020)13SCC521, 2019 (8) SCJ 253, MANU/SC/0295/2019

No. of pages in Original Judgement: 20

Case Note:

Customs - Order of discharge - Legality of - Sections 132 and 135 of the Customs Act, 1962 - Appeal maintained by Special Leave was directed against judgment of Learned Single Judge of High Court upholding dismissal of complaint filed by Appellant herein against Respondent and discharging him of offences under Sections 132 and 135 of Act, 1962 - Whether Prosecution under Sections 132 and 135(1)(a) of the Customs Act, 1962 was barred in regard to antiquities or art treasure.

Brief Facts of the case:

Appeal maintained by Special Leave is directed against judgment of Learned Single Judge of High Court upholding dismissal of complaint filed by Appellant herein against Respondent and discharging him of offences under Sections 132 and 135 of Act, 1962 The Additional Chief Metropolitan Magistrate allowed the application for discharge filed by the Respondent accepting the contention of the Respondent that there is a complete bar with regard to the prosecution under the Customs Act, 1962, and under the

Customs Act, and the Collector of Customs has power only to confiscate the goods and impose penalty for having committed breach of Section 3 of the Antiquities and Art Treasures Act, 1972 ("the Antiquities Act"). The Magistrate purported to follow the judgment of Learned Single judge of the High Court of Delhi in Dr. V.J.A. Flynn v. S.S. Chauhan and Anr. The High Court by the impugned order has come to endorse the said view.

When there is a prosecution under Section 25 of the Antiquities Act, it will not bar the imposition of confiscation and penalty in the form of monetary exaction but that does not mean that prosecution for a distinct and separate offence as contained in Section 132 of the Customs Act is in any way prohibited as being inconsistent with Section 25. In this regard though for prosecution under the Customs Act the sanctioning authority is different from the authority to sanction prosecution under the Antiquities Act, the authority to sanction prosecution under Section 26 is only qua the offence under Section 25 of the Antiquities Act. The authority competent to sanction prosecution under the Customs Act is the exclusive authority to countenance prosecution for offences under the Customs Act. So, there can be no conflict if a prosecution under Section 132 of the Customs Act is maintained after proper sanction by the competent authority under the Customs Act. It would not in any way violate either Section 25 or Section 26 of the Act.

Held,

While it may be true that the Antiquities Act is a comprehensive law, it cannot be treated as a complete or exhaustive code. Of course, the principles relating to repugnancy have been expounded in the context of conflicting claims to legislative power between two legislatures. In this case both the Customs Act 1962 and Antiquities Act have been made by Parliament.

We have expounded the ingredients of Sections 132 and 135(1)(a) of the Customs Act. The view we are taking would give full play to the Customs Act to the extent that it is not inconsistent with the Act as contemplated under Sector 4. The view which we are declaring does not do violence to the provisions of Section 25 of the Act. The contrary view which has gained acceptance at the hands of the High Court, in our view, fails to give meaning and full play as intended to the Customs Act as provided in Section 4 of the Act. Furthermore, the principle that a transaction or the same set of facts can give rise to more than one distinct offence provided the legislative intention in this regard is clear from the provisions which creates such offences cannot be lost sight of.

The upshot of the above discussion is as follows: Prosecution Under Sections 132 and 135(1)(a) of the Customs Act, 1962, is not barred in regard to the antiquities or art treasures. Accordingly, we allow the appeal and set aside the impugned order. The complaint filed may be proceeded with as per law. However, we make it very clear that pronouncement of this order shall not come in the way of the Court deciding the matter on its merits. The Court will proceed to consider the matter on its own and shall not be influenced by any observation which may have been made in this order regarding merits.

XII

Canon India Private Limited Vs.Commissioner of Customs, 20

Hon'ble Judges/Coram: S.A. Bobde, C.J.I., A.S. Bopanna and V. Ramasubramanian, JJ.

Relevant Section:

Customs Act, 1962 - Section 28(4)

Equivalent Citation: AIR2021SC1699, 2021(376)ELT3(S.C.), MANU/SC/0168/2021

No. of pages in Original Judgement: 6

Case Note:

Customs - Recovery of Duty - Show cause notice - Section 28(4) of the Customs Act, 1962 - Exemption claimed denied - Digital Still Image Video Cameras ('DSIC') - Notification No. 20/2005 dated 01.03.2005 (as amended by Notification No. 15/2012 dated 17.03.2012) - CESTAT upheld consequential confiscation, demand of interest and penalty - Hence the present appeal - Whether after clearance of the cameras on the basis that they were exempted from levy of basic Customs duty, the proceedings initiated valid in law?

Brief facts of the case:

The issue involved in the instant case is denial of exemption of basic customs duty accorded to the Digital Still Image Video Cameras ('DSIC') imported by Appellants in terms of exemption Notification No. 20/ 2005dated 01.03.2005 (as amended by Notification No. 15/2012dated 17.03.2012). The denial amounted to consequential confiscation of goods, demand of interest and imposition of penalty as provided for under various Sections of the Customs Act, 1962, which was upheld by the CESTAT. Hence, the present appeal.

The notification which purports to entrust functions as proper officer under the Customs Act has been issued by the Central Board of Excise and Customs in exercise of non-existing power Under Section 2(34) of the Customs Act. The notification is obviously invalid having been issued by an authority which had no power to do so in purported exercise of powers under a Section which does not confer any such power

Held,

It is pertinent to note that the importer had asked for a first check and had shown the cameras and the cameras were offered on 20.3.2012 along with Bill of Entry and literature detailing specifications of models. The camera could have been operated to see the length of time of the single sequence and whether recording of the single sequence exhausts the total memory of the camera (including extended memory) and whether the cameras were eligible for exemption. It is difficult in such circumstances to infer that there was any wilful misstatement of facts. In these circumstances, it must, therefore, follow that the extended period of limitation of five years was not available to any authority to re-open Under Section 28(4).

In this view of the matter, we consider it unnecessary to answer the issue whether the cameras that were cleared on the basis that they were exempted from customs duty under Exemption Notification No. 15/2012 : MANU/CUST/0071/2012 were in fact eligible for the exemption or not. The goods must be taken to have been validly cleared by the Customs officer.

We might note that cameras with similar specifications have been treated as exempted under the Explanatory Note to the Combined Nomenclature of the European communities. It is important to add that the same cameras have been considered to be eligible for exemption before 17.03.2012 and after 30.04.2015 under the exemption Notifications issued under the Customs Act read with Chapter 84 & 85 (First Schedule) of Customs Tariff Act, 1975.

In the result, these appeals are allowed. The common order dated 19.12.2017 passed by the CESTAT, New Delhi in Customs Appeal Nos. 50098, 50099, 50100 and 50280/2017 is set aside. Consequently, the impugned demand notices issued against all the three Appellants herein are also set aside.

Parties to bear their own costs.

XIII

Jaswal Neco Ltd. Vs. Commissioner of Customs, Visakhapatnam, 2015

Hon'ble Judges/Coram:A.K. Sikri and Rohinton Fali Nariman, JJ.

Relevant Section:

Customs Act 1975 - Section 3A; Section 9A, Customs Act, 1962 - Section 3, Section 12, Section 12(1), Section 14, Section 14(1), Section 14(2), Section 18, Section 18(2), Section 18(3), Section 23, Section 24, Section 25(1), Section 28AB, Section 46; Customs Tariff Act 1975 - Section 1, Section 2A, Section 3, Section 3(2), Section 3(6), Section 3A, Section 3A(2), Section 4(1), Section 8B, Section 8C, Section 9, Section 9A, Section 9A(1), Section 9A(2), Section 9A(8), Section 9(2), Section 9(2A), Section 24, Section 24(1); Finance Act, 2009 - Section 101

Equivalent Citation: 2015IX AD (S.C.) 39, 2015 (3) CCC 283 , 2015(322)ELT561(S.C.), (2015) 52 GST 755 (SC), [2015]34GSTR365(SC), 2015(8)SCALE484, (2015)17SCC769, 2015 (8) SCJ 422, MANU/SC/0827/2015

No. of pages in Original Judgement: 10

Case Note:

Customs - Exemption - Assessee imported low ash metallurgical coke - Exempt from duty if export quota met - Failed to meet whole quota - Department imposed duty which was paid by Assessee - Assessee did not pay anti-dumping duty imposed by Department - Claimed exemption under

Notification dated 19.5.2000 - Commissioner and CESTAT upheld anti-dumping duty - Whether the Assessee was exempt from anti-dumping duty under Notification dated 19.5.2000 - Whether the CESTAT was justified in increasing the rate of anti-dumping duty

Customs - Bond - Assessee furnished bond - Undertaking to pay duty for imported goods under Notifications dated 1.4.1997 and 30.4.1997 - Bond did not stipulate interest payable - Whether interest is chargeable on the duties given that Notification dated 1.4.1997 did not state that interest payable in defaultCustoms - Surcharge - Customs Act, 1962 and Customs Tariff Act, 1975 - Whether anti-dumping duty falls within special additional duty as surcharge - Whether anti-dumping duty is payable by the Assessee

Brief Facts of the case:

The Assessee engaged in the manufacture of pig iron, imported low ash metallurgical coke under seven Bills of Entry, against four advance licenses without payment of basic customs duty (BCD) , special customs duty (SCD), special additional duty (SAD) and Anti-dumping duty (ADD) during the period June 1998 to August 1998, which were exempt from duty vide various notifications. At the time of import, the Assessee furnished a bond with an undertaking to pay duty on imported goods cleared under Notification dated 1.4.1997 and 30.4.1997 in the event of failure to fulfill its export obligation. The Assessee failed to fulfill its export obligation in the terms of the exemption notifications: the entire low ash metallurgical coke imported had instead been used by the Assessee for the manufacture of pig iron. The Department raised a demand of duty of Rs. 7.21 crores.

The Assessee paid the entire duty payable towards BCD, SAD and SCD, after considering partial exports already made, but did not make any payment towards ADD. The Commissioner confirmed the duty demand of Rs. 3.37 crores and imposed a penalty of Rs.20 lakhs. Further, since the Assessee after issuance of show cause notice paid duty of Rs.1,66,18,563, the differential duty to be paid amounted to Rs. 1,70,98,510 and interest on the said amount at 24% was also held to be payable.

Held,

Doubts have been expressed about the method of computing the additional duty of customs (CVD) Under Section 3 of the Customs Tariff Act, 1975. The doubt raised is on the point that whether anti-dumping duty, safeguard duty and other duties etc. should be taken into account while computing the CVD.

In this regard, it is clarified that for computing the CVD, only the value of the imported article as determined Under Section 14 of the Customs Act, 1962, including the landing charges, if any and the basic customs duty chargeable at the rates specified in the First Schedule to the said Customs Tariff Act (read with any notification for the time being in force in respect of the basic customs duty) needs to be taken into account. Other duties such as anti-dumping duty, safeguard duty, etc. should not be taken into account.

In the explanatory notes for the last year's budget it was clarified that for computing the CVD, only the value of imported article as determined Under Section 14 of the Customs Act, 1962, including the landing charges, if any and the basic customs duty chargeable at the rates specified in the First Schedule to the Customs Tariff Act (read with any notification for the time being in force in respect of the basic customs duty) needs to be taken into account. Other duties such as anti-dumping duty, safeguard duty, etc. should not be taken into account. A view has been expressed that Section 3A of the Customs Tariff Act does not permit such interpretation. To place the matter beyond doubt, it is proposed to amend Section 3 and Section 3A of the Customs Tariff Act so as to make it very clear that for computation of additional duty of customs, only the c.i.f. price, landing charges and basic customs duty will be included. Similarly for determining special additional duty of customs (SAD), only the c.i.f. price, landing charges, basic customs duty and the additional duty of customs will be included. Other duties such as anti-dumping duty safeguard duty, etc. shall not be taken into account. This amendment will have effect from 1.3.2002.

36. Though it is stated that the object of the amendment is to clarify and set at rest doubts, it is not necessary to decide whether this amendment is clarificatory and, therefore, retrospective in view of what has already been held by us above.

As far as penalty is concerned, we feel that the Appellant before us has not diverted goods meant for export to the domestic tariff area. We are satisfied that market considerations made it difficult, if not impossible, for the Appellant to fulfill its export obligations and are, therefore, of the view that the penalty imposed in the present case ought to be set aside.

The appeal is, accordingly, allowed in the aforesaid terms and the judgment of CESTAT is set aside.

XIV

Colgate Palmolive (India) Ltd.Vs. Commissioner of Customs, Patna, 2016

Hon'ble Judges/Coram: Dipak Misra and Prafulla C. Pant, JJ.

Relevant Section:

Customs Act, 1962 - Section 8B, Section 9, Section 9A, Section 12, Section 25, Section 25(1); Customs Tariff Act 1975 - Section 2, Section 3, Section 3(1), Section 3(3), Section 3A, Section 3A(1), Section 3A(4)

Equivalent Citation: AIR2016SC4045, 2016 (3) CCC 289 , 2016(339)ELT161(S.C.), [2016]40GSTR433(SC), 2016(8)SCALE176, (2016)15SCC144, MANU/SC/0937/2016

No. of pages in Original Judgement: 10

Case Note:

Customs - Nature of Notification - Clarificatory and retrospective - Entitlement to avail exemption - Keeping in view - Need to fortify the traditional connection and strengthen - The economic cooperation - Purpose of development and mutual benefit - Government of India signed Treaty of Trade - His Majesty's Government of Nepal - July 1996 - Pursuant to aforesaid Treaty - Government of India issued Notification - Dated 23.7.1996 - Exercise of powers Under Section 25 - Customs Act, 1962 - Specified goods in notification - When imported into India from Nepal - Exempted "from the whole" of customs duty leviable - First Schedule to Customs Tariff Act, 1975 - Subject to conditions - No dispute - Appellant importing - Various dental hygiene products from Nepal - Entitled to avail exemption under the notification - Appellant availing exemption - Customs duty under the notification - In 1998, Section 3A introduced - Tariff Act provided for imposition of Special Addition Duty (SAD) - After said provision came into force - Notification issued on 01.03.2000 - Central Government prescribed rates of special duty - By said notification - After rates were prescribed - Appellant asked to pay Special Additional Duty - Paid under protest - Thereafter - Notification No. 124/2000 issued on 29.9.2000 - Amended Notification dated 23.7.1996 - Appellant filed an application - Refund of SAD - Paid in respect of imports made from Nepal - Authority concerned rejected said application - Matter came up in appeal - Customs, Excise & Gold (Control) Appellate Tribunal, Kolkata - Stand of Appellant - Notification No. 124/2000 which amended earlier notification - Enlarged the scope of exemption - Basic customs duty by including SAD - Be considered as retrospective - In view of language employed in Treaty - It was urged - All goods manufactured in Nepal - Imported into India - Exempted from customs duty - Equal to the excise duty - For the time being leviable - Similar products manufactured in India - As per the Treaty, no SAD was leviable - Hence, notification dated 29.09.2000 was clarificatory in nature - Further contended - Levy of SAD after rates were fixed - Contrary to terms of Treaty - It was rectified by issuing Notification No. 124/2000 - Therefore, Appellant entitled to refund of amount - Paid towards SAD - Further argued - Notification was retrospective in nature - Revenue resisted stand of Appellant-Assessee - Prior to 29.9.2000 - SAD was correctly levied - In respect of imports - There is no justification - Treating the Notification as retrospective - Member (Judicial) observed - Exemption notification - Could not be considered having retrospective effect - Any exemption provision - Enlarges the scope of earlier Notification - Cannot be considered clarificatory - Further opined - Earlier notification did not remotely suggest - Exemption from basic customs duty included - Exemption from SAD - Earlier notification exempted from basic custom duty - Latter from SAD - Learned Member (Judicial) dismissed appeal - Member (Technical) expressed dissent - Opined - Once a Treaty entered by Central Government - Issue of notification - Under provisions of Customs Act, 1962 - Ministerial Act - Notification dated 29.9.2000 - A belated response to effectuate terms of Treaty - Learned Member (Technical) observed - If it was a simplicitor amendment - Exempt or reduce the rates - Certain specified imports - An amendment required to be made - Notification dated 01.03.2000 - Not to

Notification dated 23.7.1996 - That having been not done - It can be safely concluded - There was a belated reference - Real intention - To give retrospectivity to notification - Learned Member (Technical) opined - Matter be referred to larger bench for decision - As there was difference of opinion - Matter was placed before third member (Technical) - Third Member held - Both notifications are independent - Both would be applicable - From date they had been issued - Do not remotely suggest any retrospectivity - Further opined - No ambiguity in earlier or subsequent notification - He agreed with Member (Judicial) - Appeal stood dismissed - Hence, Present appeals - Whether exemption notification issued on 29th September, 2000 is clarificatory in nature - Whether the issue of notification was a formal ministerial act which got delayed for administrative reasons - Whether the SAD notification was retrospective in nature.

Brief Facts of the case:

Keeping in view the need to fortify the traditional connection and strengthen the economic cooperation for the purpose of development and mutual benefit, the Government of India had signed the Treaty of Trade with His Majesty's Government of Nepal in July, 1996.

Pursuant to aforesaid Treaty, the Government of India issued a Notification dated 23.7.1996, in exercise of powers Under Section 25 of the Customs Act, 1962 (the Customs Act) whereby specified goods in the notification when imported into India from Nepal were exempted "from the whole" of the customs duty leviable under the First Schedule to the Customs Tariff Act, 1975 (the Tariff Act) subject to the conditions, if any, specified in the corresponding entry in column (3) of the Table to the notification. There is no dispute that the Appellant who was importing various dental hygiene products from Nepal was entitled to avail exemption under the notification. As the factual matrix would unveil, it was availing the exemption from the customs duty under the notification.

In 1998, Section 3A was introduced in the Tariff Act which provided for imposition of special additional duty. After the said provision came into force, a Notification was issued on 01.03.2000. By the said notification the Central Government prescribed the rates of special duty.

Held,

Decisions in the case of ***W.P.I.L. Limited v. Commissioner, Central Excise***MANU/SC/0122/2005 : 2005 (181) ELT 259 SC and ***Ralson India Limited v. Commissioner of Central Excise, Chandigarh***MANU/SC/0597/2015 : 2015

(319) ELT 234 SC do not assist the Appellant. In the said authorities, the contention of the Assessee was accepted on the ground that both power driven pumps as well as parts of power driven pump had for long remained exempt. However, when earlier notifications were rescinded in order to consolidate and reduce the number of notifications and then the new notification was issued on 1st March, 1994 then by mistake and erroneously parts of power driven pump were not included, whereas manufacture of power driven pumps was included. In this context, it was held that the subsequent notification including parts of power driven pump was merely clarificatory and when clarificatory notifications are issued, they have retrospective effect. The instant case is not suggestive of any mistake or error or even inadvertence. The plea that there was delay in issue of notification, exempting special additional duty is not acceptable. It is because, what was earlier exempted under the protocol was basic customs duty and also additional customs duty equal to the duty of excise in some cases and on satisfying the conditions stipulated and it did not deal and relate to special additional duty chargeable Under Section 3A of the Tariff Act, which had introduced a new duty altogether. Therefore, we repel the submission that the exemption notification issued on 29th September, 2000 is clarificatory. It was intended to be applied prospectively. That apart, it cannot be also said the issue of notification was a formal ministerial act which got delayed for administrative reasons. It was a conscious act and a deliberate decision which came into existence after due deliberation when it was decided to grant exemption Under Section 3A of the Tariff Act.

In view of our foregoing analysis, we find no merit in the appeals preferred by the Assessee and accordingly dismiss them without any order as to costs.

XV

Commissioner of Customs, Mumbai Vs. Aban Loyd Chiles Offshore Ltd. and Ors., 2017

Hon'ble Judges/Coram: Dipak Misra and Prafulla C. Pant, JJ.

Relevant Section:

CUSTOMS ACT, 1962 - Section 2

Equivalent Citation: 2017 (1) CCC 185 , 2017(346)ELT513(S.C.), (2017) 60 GST 207 (SC), [2017]43GSTR166(SC), (2017)2MLJ610, 2017(2)SCALE183, (2017)3SCC211, 2017 (6) SCJ 696, MANU/SC/0105/2017

No. of pages in Original Judgement: 10

Case Note:

Customs - Vessel entering into territorial waters - Repairs - Confiscation - Customs Act, 1962 - Assessee/first Respondent obtained approval of Government for import of Rig - Special Import Licence was granted - As per special instructions of Letter of Credit, shipping document should indicate place of final destination and should not be different from port of discharge - Rig was towed into waters and after it was repaired, taken out of territorial waters - Investigations by Customs authorities into these two cases of importation led them to conclude that there had been contravention of certain provisions by Assessee - Notice was issued to Assessee alleging that imports that took place during period in question were contrary to provisions of law - From confiscation of rig to demand of duty were proposed - Commissioner held that rig was carried and brought on three occasions - It was not declared in Import General Manifest of towing rigs, as was required - Rig was ordered for confiscation with option of redeeming it by payment of fine and duty was also demanded - Penalties were also imposed - Assessee preferred appeal before Tribunal - Tribunal held that each of three clauses of extended definition applied to different fact situations, and each of these situations requires to be considered on its own merits - It concluded that in circumstances payment of duty on rig did not arise and even if the rig was liable to duty - It opined that provisions of Act would be attracted and, therefore, contravention of clause had been established - Also held that goods were unloaded without permission of competent authority - Tribunal opined that rig was liable for confiscation - However, it opined that as there was no deliberate intention on part of importer to contravene Regulations although there was clear negligence and Rules were not followed - Fine for redemption of rig was reduced - Hence, present appeals - Whether order passed by Tribunal was sustainable

Brief facts of the case:

The Assessee/first Respondent, engaged in business of offshore oil and gas exploratory drilling and related activities on contract basis, inter alia, for the Oil and Natural Gas Corporation Limited (ONGC) had obtained the approval of the Government of India for the import of a Rig for such oil field services. It was granted a Special Import Licence for the import of the said Rig along with certain drilling equipments. A confirmed irrevocable Letter of Credit for the shipment of Capital goods was given by ICICI Bombay against the said Import Licence. As per the special instructions of that Letter of Credit, the transport documents were required to fulfil six conditions including the one, that was, the shipping document should indicate the place of final destination and should not be different from the port of discharge. The Assessee purchased a rig. The rig was towed directly to the drilling site. The importer wrote to the Commissioner of Customs seeking permission to import the rig into the city for carrying out repairs and re-export in terms of the provisions of Notification.

Held,

The authorities have laid emphasis on the factum that the rig was purchased for being used in the oil field of ONGC and for this purpose the owner had made an application and permission/licence for import was granted by the Ministry of Industry. The rig was purchased from foreign exchange released by the Government on the basis of the import licence for the rig. If the rig was not to be used in India, foreign exchange would not have been released and import licence would not have been granted. This argument on behalf of the department does not further the stand. It cannot be regarded as conclusive. Release of foreign exchange, approval and licence, etc. are prior to the import. Import may not take place in spite of this aforesaid clearances/licence and release of foreign exchange. There may have been violation of another enactment/provision as the rig was not imported, albeit for deciding the question whether the rig was imported into India, the requirement of home consumption has to be satisfied. Then alone, the 'good', i.e., the vessel/rig would be taxable and customs duty payable under the Act. Pertinently, the adjudication order does not hold that the import had taken place in 1987 when the rig first put into operation in the high seas. This was not treated as the date of import or home consumption. The import as per the authorities had taken place when the rig was brought for repairs. The evaluation of the rig has been done on the basis of the last visit of the rig for repair in 1998.

While we are disposed to accept that there was no import, we would not on the said finding hold that the owner had not violated the provisions of the Act, which are much broader and wider in scope. The Act regulates and mandates compliance by the foreign going vessels when they enter the territorial waters. Provisions of the Act are required to be met and complied with even when no goods are to be unloaded for import into India or the vessel is not a 'good' meant for home consumption. Thus, violations recorded by the tribunal cannot be found fault with.

Thus analysed, we are of the indubitable opinion, that the decision rendered by the tribunal deserves our concurrence and we so do. Consequently, all the appeals are dismissed without any order as to costs.

XVI

Commissioner of Customs, Bangalore-1 Vs. Motorola India Ltd., 2019

Hon'ble Judges/Coram: Arun Mishra, M.R. Shah and B.R. Gavai, JJ.

Relevant Section:

Customs Act, 1962 - Section 130; Section 130E

Equivalent Citation: 2019(5)BLJ351, 2019(5)CTC727, 2019(368)ELT3(S.C.), 2019(11)SCALE803, (2019)9SCC563, MANU/SC/1210/2019

No. of pages in Original Judgement: 5

Case Note:

Customs - Filing of appeal - Jurisdiction thereto - Sections 130 and 130E of Customs Act, 1962 - Commissioner held that Assessee was liable to pay customs duty along with interest and penalty - Being aggrieved thereby, Assessee preferred appeal before Tribunal, Tribunal allowed appeal - Being aggrieved thereby, Commissioner preferred appeal before High Court under Section 130 of Act - Division Bench held that appeal under Section 130 of Act was not tenable before High Court but would be tenable under Section 130E of Act before this Court - Hence, present appeal - Whether appeal from order of Tribunal would lie before High Court under Section 130 of Act or to this Court under Section 130E of Act.

Brief facts of the case:

The Commissioner passed an order in original, holding that the Assessee was liable to pay the customs duty along with interest and penalty. Being aggrieved thereby, the Assessee preferred an appeal before the Tribunal. The Tribunal allowed the appeal. Being aggrieved thereby, the Commissioner preferred an appeal before the High Court under the provisions of Section 130 of the Customs Act. The Division Bench of the High Court, held that the appeal under Section 130 of the Customs Act was not tenable before the High Court but would be tenable under Section 130E of the Customs Act before this Court.

Upon a conjoint reading of the Section 130 and Section 130E of the Customs Act, 1962, it could thus be seen that an appeal shall lie to the High Court against every order passed in appeal by the Appellate Tribunal, if the High Court is satisfied that the case involves a substantial question of law. The only exception carved out is that an appeal shall lie before this Court and shall not lie before the High Court against the order relating, amongst other things, to the determination of any question having relation to the rate of duty of customs or to the value of goods for the purposes of assessment.

Held,

We are of the considered view that the Legislature has carved out only following categories of cases to which it has intended to give a special treatment of providing an appeal directly to this Court.

(i) determination of a question relating to a rate of duty;

(ii) determination of a question relating to the valuation of goods for the purpose of assessment;

(iii) determination of a question relating to the classification of goods under the Tariff and whether or not they are covered by an exemption notification;

(iv) whether the value of goods for purposes of assessment should be enhanced or reduced having regard to certain matters that the said Act provides for.

Reverting to the present case, it could clearly be seen that the only question that is involved is whether the Assessee had violated the conditions of the exemption notification by not utilizing the imported materials for manufacturing of the declared final product and was, therefore, liable for payment of duty, interest and penalty. Neither any question with regard to determination of rate of duty arises nor a question relating to valuation of goods for the purposes of assessment arises in the present case. The appeals also do not involve determination of any question relating to the classification of goods, nor do they involve the question as to whether they are covered by the exemption notification or not. Undisputedly, the goods are covered by the said notification. The only question is as to whether the Assessee has breached the conditions which are imposed by the notification for getting exemption from payment of the customs duty or not. The appeals do not involve any question of law of general public importance which would be applicable to a class or category of Assessees as a whole. The question is purely inter-se between the parties and is required to be adjudicated upon the facts available.

In that view of the matter, we find that the High Court was not justified in holding that the appeals are not maintainable Under Section 130 of the Customs Act but are tenable before this Court Under Section 130E of the Customs Act.

In the result, the appeals are allowed and the impugned orders passed by the High Court are set aside. The appeals are remitted back to the High Court for de novo consideration of the appeals on their own merits.

In the facts and circumstances of the case, there shall be no order as to costs.

XVII

Commissioner of Customs Vs. Atul Automations Pvt. Ltd. and Ors., 2019

Hon'ble Judges/Coram: Ranjan Gogoi, C.J.I., Navin Sinha and K.M. Joseph, JJ.

Relevant Section:

Customs Act, 1962 - Section 125; Section 112(a), Section 114AA

Equivalent Citation: 2019(365)ELT465(S.C.), 2019(9)FLT184, 2019(1)SCALE686, (2019)3SCC539, 2019 (10) SCJ 390, MANU/SC/0067/2019

No. of pages in Original Judgement: 4

Case Note:

Customs - Release of goods - Direction - Sections 3 and 5 of the Foreign Trade Act, 1992; Section 11, 125 of Customs Act, 1962; Section 11(8) and (9) read with Rule 17(2) of Foreign Trade (Regulation) Rules, 1993 - Appeal was against order of High Court holding that, MFDs were not prohibited but restricted items for import and directed release of goods subject to execution of a simple bond without sureties for 90% of enhanced assessed value - Whether impugned order of High Court directing release of goods was sustainable.

Brief Facts of the case:

Respondents during October-November, 2016 imported certain consignments of Multi-Function Devices (Digital Photocopiers and Printers)

(MFDs). Commissioner of Customs held that, imports were in violation of Foreign Trade Policy framed under Foreign Trade (Development and Regulation) Act, 1992 and Rule 15(1)(2) of Hazardous and Other Wastes (Management and Transboundary Movement) Rules, 2016. Redemption fine was imposed under Section 125 of Customs Act, 1962 and consignment released for re-export only. Penalty was also imposed under Section 112(a) along with penalty under Section 114AA of Customs Act as also penalty was imposed on Directors. In appeal before the Tribunal, Tribunal held that, MFDs did not constitute "waste" under Rule 3(1)(23) of Waste Management Rules and had a utility life of 5 to 7 years, as certified by Chartered Engineer. Release of consignment was directed under Section 125 of Customs Act as Respondents were held to have substantially complied with requirements of Rule 13 of Waste Management Rules read with Schedule VIII Entry 4(j) except for country of origin certificate. Tribunal further noticed that, earlier also similar consignments of Respondent and others had been released at Calcutta, Chennai and Cochin ports upon payment of redemption fine. Redemption fine was reduced as also penalty under Section 112(a) of Customs Act was reduced including that on Director also. Penalty under Section 114AA was done away with. In appeal preferred by Revenue, High Court held that, MFDs correctly fell in category of "other wastes" under Rule 3(1)(23) of Waste Management Rules read with Part B and Part D of Schedule III Item B1110 dealing with used Multi-Function Printer and Copying Machines. Adverting to provisions of Foreign Trade Act and Foreign Trade Policy framed thereunder, it was held that, MFDs were not prohibited but restricted items for import. Section 11(8) and (9) of Foreign Trade Act provided for confiscation and redemption of goods imported without authorisation upon payment of market value. Order for release of goods was upheld subject to execution of a simple bond without sureties for 90% of enhanced assessed value, with further liberty to Director General of Foreign Trade (the DGFT), along with directions.

Held,

Rule 13(2) provides the procedure for import of other wastes listed in Part D Schedule III. Item B1110 of the Schedule mentions used Multifunction Print and Copying Machines (MFDs). Entry 4(j) lists out five documents required for import of used MFDs. The Respondents have been found to be substantially compliant in this regard and the requirement for the country of origin certificate has been found to be vague by the High Court. Form 6 has rightly been held to be not applicable to the subject goods.

Rule 15 of the Waste Management Rules dealing with illegal traffic, provides that import of "other wastes" shall be deemed illegal if it is without permission from the Central Government under the Rules and is required to be re-exported. Significantly the Customs Act does not provide for re-export. The Central Government under the Foreign Trade Policy has not prohibited but restricted the import subject to authorisation. The High Court therefore rightly held that the MFDs having a utility period, the Extended Producer Responsibility would arise only after the utility period was over. In any event, the E-waste Rules 2016 certificate had since been issued to the Respondents by the Central Pollution Control Board before the goods have been cleared.

We therefore find no reason to interfere with the impugned orders. In the statutory scheme of the Foreign Trade Act as discussed, we further find no error in the penultimate direction to the Respondents for deposit of bond without sureties for 90% of the enhanced valuation of the goods leaving it to the DGFT to decide whether confiscation needs to be ordered or release be granted on redemption at the market value, in which event the Respondents shall be entitled to set off.

The appeals are dismissed.

XVIII

Indusind Media & Communications Ltd. Vs. Commissioner of Customs, New Delhi, 2019

Hon'ble Judges/Coram: U.U. Lalit and Vineet Saran, JJ.

Relevant Sections:

Customs Act, 1962 - Section 14, Section 14(1A), Section 18, Section 111, Section 111(m), Section 112(a), Section 114AA, Section 125, Section 130E, Section 156; Customs Tariff Act, 1975; Customs Valuation (determination Of Price Of Imported Goods) Rules, 1988 - Rule 3, Rule 4, Rule 5, Rule 6, Rule 7, Rule 8, Rule 9, Rule 9(1), Rule 10A; Rule 10

Equivalent Citation: AIR2019SC4812, 2019(368)ELT235(S.C.), 2019(13)SCALE124, (2019)17SCC108, MANU/SC/1345/2019

No. of pages in Original Judgement: 7

Case Note:

Customs - Penalty - Mis-declaration of valuation - Sections 111 and 114AA of Customs Act, 1962 - Appellant imported certain goods and filed Bill of Entry - Show Cause Notice was issued by Department stating inter alia that Importer had fabricated documents by way of splitting of value of goods and declared lesser value with sole intention to evade payment of

Customs Duties - Commissioner observed that Appellant had intentionally not declared true and correct value and correct classification of imported goods and imposed penalty under Section 114AA of Act - On appeal before Tribunal, Tribunal held that In view of mis-declaration established in respect of valuation, imported goods will be liable for confiscation under Section 111 of Act and Appellant would also be liable for penalty - Hence, present appeal - Whether impugned order of confiscation and imposition of penalty under Section 114AA of Act warrant any interference.

Brief facts of the case:

The Appellant imported certain goods at air cargo complex, New Delhi and filed Bill of Entry. Show Cause Notice was issued by the Department stating inter alia that the Importer had fabricated documents by way of splitting of value of the goods and declared lesser value to the Customs Department with the sole intention to evade payment of Customs Duties. Commissioner rejected the declaration by the Appellant. It was observed that the Appellant had intentionally not declared the true and correct value and correct classification of imported goods and imposed penalty under Section 114AA of the Customs Act, 1962. Appellant, being aggrieved, filed Customs Appeal before the Tribunal. The Tribunal held that in view of the mis-declaration established in respect of valuation, the imported goods would be liable for confiscation under Section 111 of the Customs Act and the Appellant would also be liable for penalty.

Held,

The subsequent decisions of this Court in Commissioner of Customs, Ahmedabad v. Essar Steel Ltd. MANU/SC/0427/2015 : 2015 (319) ELT 202 : (2015) 8 SCC 175, and in Commissioner of Customs (Import), Mumbai v. Hindalco Industries Ltd. MANU/SC/0657/2015 : (2015) 320 ELT 42 (SC) : (2015) 14 SCC 750 have followed the same principle that technical agreements involved in said cases pertained to post-importation activity. To similar effect was the conclusion by this Court in an earlier decision in Commissioner of Customs, New Delhi v. Prodelin India (P) Ltd. MANU/SC/3805/2006 : 2006 (202) ELT A130 : (2006) 10 SCC 280 that technical know how fee was in respect of post-importation activities and could not be added to the value of the imported goods.

It is a matter of record that after considering the purchase order in the instant case, the Tribunal found that apart from supply of equipment, necessary software had to be embedded in the equipment before the supply was effected. The facts also disclose that out of 19 items indicated in the

Bill of Entry, only 8 items were physically presented while the rest were already embedded in the main unit. These facts are not only reflective that the individual components were intended to contribute together and attain a clearly defined function as dealt with in Note 4 of Section XVI as stated above, but also indicate that software that was embedded through cards in the main unit, was not any post-importation activity. The value of the software and the concerned services were therefore rightly included and taken as part of the importation.

The facts on record as stated above further disclose that the Department was therefore right in invoking principle under said Note 4 and considering the imported items as part of one apparatus or machine to be classifiable under the heading appropriate to the function. The submission advanced by the Appellant in that behalf therefore has to be rejected.

Rule 9(1)(b) of 1988 Rules as quoted above in the decision in Toyota Kirloskar MANU/SC/2855/2007 : 2007 (213) ELT 4 (SC) : (2007) 5 SCC 371, case shows that the value in respect of "materials, components, parts and similar items incorporated in the imported goods" has to be added while determining the transaction value. Said Rule 9 is almost identical to Rule 10 of 2007 Rules. Thus, even if the governing Rule is taken to be Rule 9 of 1988 Rules, there would be no difference in the ultimate analysis.

Consequently, we do not find any merit in the present appeal. Affirming the view taken by the Tribunal, we dismiss this appeal, without any order as to costs.

XIX

Wipro Ltd. Vs. Assistant Collector of Customs and Ors., 2015

Hon'ble Judges/Coram: A.K. Sikri and Rohinton Fali Nariman, JJ.

Relevant Section:

CUSTOMS ACT, 1962 - Section 14; Section 14(1-A)

Equivalent Citation: 2015VI AD (S.C.) 98, 2015 (2) CCC 175 , 2015(319)ELT177(S.C.), (2015) 52 GST 47 (SC), [2015]32GSTR504(SC), (2015)5MLJ232(SC), 2015(3)RCR(Civil)478, 2015(5)SCALE390, (2015)14SCC161, 2015 (5) SCJ 424, MANU/SC/0468/2015

No. of pages in Original Judgement: 10

Case Note:

Constitution - Validity of amendment - Addition of value - Sections 14(1) and 14(1-A) of Customs Act, 1962 and Article 14 of Constitution of India - Present appeals challenging constitutional validity of proviso (ii) to Rule 9(2) introduced vide Notification as same entitled authorities to add 1% of F.O.B. value of goods on account of loading, unloading and handling charges - Whether impugned proviso was ultra vires to Section 14(1) and Section 14(1-A) of Act, 1962 - Held, impugned proviso was against objective behind Section 14 namely to accept actual cost paid or payable and even in absence thereof to arrive at cost which is most proximate to actual cost - Addition of 1% of free on board value was thus, in circumstance, clearly arbitrary and irrational and would be violative of Article 14 of Constitution

- Only justification for stipulating 1% of F.O.B. value was that it would help customs authorities to apply rate uniformly - Said could be justification only if loading, unloading and handling charges were not ascertainable - Where such charges were known and determinable, there was no reason to have such yardstick - Therefore, authorities had not been able to satisfy as to how such provision helped in achieving object of Section 14 of Act - Further, loading, unloading and handling charges were fixed by International Airport Authority - Therefore, impugned amendment was unsustainable and bad in law - Appeal allowed.

Held,

It is very common for the legislature to provide for a general rule-making power to carry out the purpose of the Act. When such a power is given, it may be permissible to find out the object of the enactment and then see if the rules framed satisfy the test of having been so framed as to fall within the scope of such general power confirmed. If the rule-making power is not expressed in such a usual general form then it shall have to be seen if the rules made are protected by the limits prescribed by the parent act. (See: Sant Saran Lal v. ParsuramSahu MANU/SC/0036/1965 : AIR 1966 SC 1852). From the provisions of the Act we cannot spell out any legislative intent delegating expressly, or by necessary implication, the power to enact any prohibition on transfer of land. We are also in agreement with the submission of Shri Anil Divan that by placing complete prohibition on transfer of land subservient to tea estates no purpose sought to be achieved by the Act is advanced and so also such prohibition cannot be sustained. Land forming part of a tea estate including land subservient to a tea plantation have been placed beyond the ken of the Act. Such land is not to be taken in account either for calculating area of surplus land or for calculating the area of land which a person may retain as falling within the ceiling limit. We fail to understand how a restriction on transfer of such land is going to carry out any purpose of the Act. We are fortified in taking such view by the Constitution Bench decision of this Court in Bhim Singhji v. Union of India MANU/SC/0509/1980 : (1981) 1 SCC 166 whereby Sub-section (1) of Section 27 of the Urban Land (Ceiling and Regulation) Act, 1976 was struck down as invalid insofar as it imposed a restriction on transfer of any urban of urbanisable land with a building or a portion only of such building which was within the ceiling area. The provision impugned therein imposed a restriction on transactions by way of sale, mortgage, gift or lease of vacant land or buildings for a period exceeding ten years, or otherwise for a period of ten years from the date of the commencement of the Act even though such vacant land, with or without a building thereon, fell within the ceiling limits. The Constitution Bench held (by majority) that such property will be transferable without the constraints mentioned in Sub-section (1) of Section 27 of the said Act. Their Lordships opined that the light to carry on a business guaranteed Under Article 19(1)(g) of the Constitution carried with it the right not to carry on business. It logically followed, as a necessary corollary, that the right to acquire, hold and dispose of property guaranteed to citizen Under Article 19(1)(f) carried with it the right not to hold any property. It is difficult to appreciate how a citizen could be compelled to own property against his will though he wanted to alienate it and the land being within the ceiling limits was outside the purview of Section 3 of the Act and that being so the person owning the land was not governed by any of the provisions of the Act. Reverting back to the case at hand, the learned Counsel for the State of Himachal Pradesh has not been able to satisfy us as to how such a prohibition as is imposed by the impugned amendment in the Rules helps in achieving the object of the Act.

We are also of the opinion that a delegated power to legislate by making rules "for carrying out the purposes of the Act" is a general delegation without laying down any guidelines; it cannot be so exercised as to bring into existence substantive rights or obligations or disabilities not contemplated by the provisions of the Act itself.

36. We are, therefore, of the opinion that impugned amendment, namely, proviso (ii) to Sub-rule (2) of Rule 9 introduced vide Notification dated 05.07.1990 is unsustainable and bad in law as it exists in the present form and it has to be read down to mean that this clause would apply only when actual charges referred to in Clause (b) are not ascertainable.

As a result, judgment of the High Court is set aside and the appeals are allowed in the aforesaid terms with no order as to cost.

XX

Star Industries Vs. Commissioner of Customs (Imports) Raigad, 2015

Hon'ble Judges/Coram: A.K. Sikri and Rohinton Fali Nariman, JJ.

Relevant Sections:

Customs Act 1962 - Section 2, Section 3, Section 3(1); Section 25, Section 28, Section 28AA, Section 28(1), Section 108, Section 110, Section 111, Section 112, Section 114A, Section 125

Equivalent Citation: 2015XII AD (S.C.) 239, 2015(324)ELT656(S.C.), (2015) 52 GST 922 (SC), [2015]35GSTR402(SC), 2015(10)SCALE529, (2016)2SCC362, 2016 (2) SCJ 75, MANU/SC/1150/2015

No. of pages in Original Judgement: 10

Case Note:

Customs - Exemption from payment of CVD - Appellant engaged in manufacture of Ferro-Alloys - One of inputs - Roasted Molybdenum Ore/ Concentrate - Assessee regularly importing Ore concentrate - Claiming benefit of Notification No. 4/2006-CE - No CVD levied - Directorate of Revenue - Roasted Molybdenum Ore - Different from 'ores' - Benefit not available - Consignments seized - Assessee agreed to pay CVD - Also paid differential duty - Show cause notice issued - Adjudication - Order passed confirming demand - Order challenged - CESTAT concurred with adjudicating authority - Partial relief granted - Appeal against CESTAT order - Whether 'Ore Concentrate' imported by the Assessee can be treated as 'Ores' mentioned in Notification No. 4/2006 - Whether Molybdenum Ore after it undergoes the process of being roasted and come to be known as Ore Concentrate still remains Ores - Whether the Ore Concentrates imported by the Assessee is eligible for complete exemption from payment of additional duty of custom/CVD under Notification No.4/2006-CE

Brief Facts of the case:

The Appellant (Assessee) is engaged in the manufacture of Ferro-Alloys falling under Chapter 72 of Central Excise Tariff. One of the inputs for manufacture of Ferro-Alloys is Roasted Molybdenum Ore/Concentrate. The Assessee has been regularly importing the aforesaid material i.e. Roasted Molybdenum Ore/Concentrate (Ore Concentrate).

The import of Ore Concentrate is, otherwise, subject to additional duty of custom, i.e. countervailing duty (CVD) in addition to normal custom duty. Vide Notification No. 4/2006-CE dated March 01, 2011, which is a general exemption notification, various items, either fully or partially, exempted from payment of excise duty. One of the items described in this notification is 'Ores' and the excise duty payable is Nil.

The Assessee has been regularly importing Ore Concentrate and claiming the benefit of the aforesaid Notification No. 4/2006-CE. The Customs Department had been extending this benefit. As a result, no CVD was levied. However, the Directorate of Revenue Intelligence (DRI) received some information indicating that the Assessee was misdeclaring the product as 'Molybdenum Ore' or 'Roasted Molybdenum Ore' and on that basis, seeking benefit of exemption under Notification No. 4/2006-CE. According to them, Roasted Molybdenum Ore was, in fact, Ore Concentrate which was different from 'Ores' and, therefore, benefit of said Notification was not available to the Assessee. Based on this, two imported consignments of the Assessee were detained for examination. Examination of the goods revealed that one consignment of bags, in which the goods were packed, contained labels/ marking which read as 'Roasted Molybdenum Concentrate'. In respect of the other consignment, the markings were 'Molybdenum Sulfide (MoS2) Roasted. Samples of the products under importation were drawn and sent for chemical examination to Chemical Examiner, CRCL, Vadodara. On that basis, the goods/consignment was seized under the provisions of Section 110 of the Customs Act, 1962 on the reasonable plea that they are liable to confiscation Under Section 111 of the said Act.

Held,

The Customs Tariff Act, 1975 was preceded by the Indian Tariff Act, 1934. Section 2A of the Tariff Act, 1934 provided for levy of countervailing duty. This section stipulated that any article which was imported into India shall be liable to customs duty equal to the excise duty for the time being leviable on a like article if produced or manufactured in India. In the notes to clauses to the Customs Tariff Bill 1975 with regard to Clause 3 it was stated that "Clause 3 provides for the levy of additional duty on an imported article to counter-balance the excise duty leviable on the like article made indigenously, or on the indigenous raw materials, components or ingredients which go into the making of the like indigenous article. This provision corresponds to Section 2A of the existing Act, and is necessary to safeguard the interests of the manufacturers in India." Apart from the plain language of the Customs Tariff Act, 1975 even the notes to clauses show the legislative intent of providing for a charging section in the Tariff Act, 1975 for enabling the levy of additional duty to be equal to the amount of excise duty leviable on a like article if produced or manufactured in India. Even though the impost Under Section 3 is not called a countervailing duty, there can be little doubt that this levy Under Section 3 of the Customs Tariff Act has been enacted to provide for a level playing field to the present or future manufacturers of the like articles in India.

(Emphasis supplied)

This object of levy has to be kept in mind while interpreting notification No. 4/2006-CE for the purposes of levy of CVD on concentrates. If the domestic manufacturer of concentrates is liable to pay excise duty on conversion of 'ores' into 'concentrates' in terms of Note 4 to Chapter 26, can his interests be sub-served when concentrates imported into India are not levied to CVD at the same rate by interpretation of Notification No. 4/2006 so as to construe that ores includes 'concentrates' and, therefore, no CVD is leviable. In our humble view, such an interpretation militates against the interests of domestic producers and also the plain language of the notification. Accordingly we hold that the benefit of exemption under Notification No. 4/2006-CE will not be applicable to 'concentrates' imported from abroad.

35. It was submitted by the learned Counsel for the Assessee that the entire exercise is Revenue neutral because of the reason that the Assessee would, in any case, get CENVAT credit of the duty paid. If that is so, this argument in the instant case rather goes against the Assessee. Since the

Assessee is in appeal and if the exercise is Revenue neutral, then there was no need even to file the appeal. Be that as it may, if that is so, it is always open to the Assessee to claim such a credit.

We, thus, do not find any merit in this appeal and dismiss the same with cost.

VIDEOS & TV SHOWS ON LAW & EXIM

List of some important videos & TV shows on Law & EXIM by Adv. Jayprakash Somani on his YouTube Channel 'Jayprakash Somani EXIM & Legal'

Legal Videos: Hindi -English

1) SLP in Supreme Court / Special Leave Petitions in the Supreme Court of India

2) Transfer of Civil & Criminal Cases by the Supreme Court of India / Transfer of Matrimonial Cases

3) Appellate Jurisdiction of the Supreme Court of India

4) Jurisdictions of the Supreme Court of India

5) Public Interest Litigation in the Supreme Court of India / PIL in Supreme Court

6) Article 32 Writ Petitions in the Supreme Court of India

7) Bail Matters Top 10 Supreme Court Cases

8) FIR Quashing in High Court & Supreme Court

9) Bail & Anticipatory Bail Matters in Supreme Court

10) Insolvency & Bankruptcy Matters in the Supreme Court

11) Insolvency & Bankruptcy Code 2016 Part 1

12) Insolvency & Bankruptcy Code 2016 Part 2

13) Insolvency & Bankruptcy Code 2016 Part 3

14) Corporate Liquidation Process

15) Supreme Court Rules & Procedures Webinar of 2.5 hour on Zoom

16) RDDBFI Act, 1993 (Introduction)

17) The Indian Contact Act 1872

18) Negotiable Instruments Act (Introduction)

19) How to avoid matrimonial disputes& some more videos

20)SEBI Matters in the Supreme Court

21) Matrimonial Matters: Supreme Court's 20 Case Laws

22) Consumer Matters Supreme Court's 20 Case Laws

23) Service Matters Supreme Court's 20 Case Laws

24) How to Search Lawyer for Your Matter

25) Property Matters Supreme Court's 20 Case Laws

26) Bail Matters: Supreme Court's 20 Case Laws

27) Supreme Court / High Court Vacation Benches

28)69000 Teacher's Recruitment Matters of UP Government in the Supreme Court

29) Contempt of Court Matters in the Supreme Court

30) Advocate Act's Matters in the Supreme Court

31) Business Law Matters in the Supreme Court

32) Banking Matters in the Supreme Court

33) Labour Law Matters in the Supreme Court

34) Arbitration Matters in the Supreme Court

35) Careers in Law -Zoom Webinar by Adv. Jayprakash Somani

36) Civil Matters in the Supreme Court

37) Consumer Protection Act | Consumer Matters in the Supreme Court

38) Corporate Matters in the Supreme Court

39) Criminal Matters in the Supreme Court

40) Role of Respondent in the Supreme Court of India

41) Motor Vehicle Accident Matters in Supreme Court with case laws

42) Article 131 Original Suits in Supreme Court

43)PIL in Supreme Court/ Public Interest Litigations in the Supreme Court of India'

44)CAB Citizenship Amendment Bill is not Unconstitutional

45) Supreme Court of India Cases & Process – Marathi

46) Legal Services Export / Export of Legal Services

47) Transfer of Matrimonial Cases by the Supreme Court of India

48) Public Interest Litigation PIL

49) The Specific Relief Act (Introduction)

50) Corporate Insolvency Resolution Process CIRP

51)ABMM's Career 5 - Careers in Law

52) Transfer of cases by Supreme Court

53) Writ Petitions in High Court & Supreme Court of India

54) Supreme Court Jurisdictions - Appeals, SLP, Writ Petitions, Transfer, Original, Review, Curative

55)LEGAL INDIA TV Show: Cases Handled in Supreme Court

56) Corporate Liquidation Process

57) Legal Services Export / Export of Legal Services

EXIM Videos: Hindi -English

1) Yes, I can do Import Export Business Easily! 36 points excellent video in Hindi

2) Yes, I can do Import Export Business Easily! 36 points excellent video in English

3) Import Export Business – Hindi video

4) Import Export Business - English video

5) Export Import Marathi TV Interview

6) Scope for Commerce Students in International Business- TV Show

7) Scope for Management Student in International Business- TV Show

8) Scope for Engineering Students in International Business – TV Show

9) Women in International Business- TV Show

10) How to do Import Export Business Successfully!'

11) Where one can get full information on Import Export Business?

12) What to do import & export?

13) Import Export Workshop/ Training/Course/ Diploma

14) How to Start Import Export Business & How to grow it. Live Webinar

15) Success Stories & Failure Stories in Import & Export Business

16) For MSME Scope in Export & Import...

17) Exports In Agri. & Food Products – English & some more videos

18) Exports to Dubai, Aabudhabii. e. UAE

19) Jewellery Exports from India

20) How to attend EXIM workshop to become excellent Exporter

21) Import Export Best Training Course – Online & Offline

22) Agri Product Export

23) Scope for Woman in International Business

24) Management Graduates Scope in International Business

25) Pharma Product's Export

26) Best Import Export Course | Practical Training | Aaronica Global Exim

27) Import Export Business for Commerce Graduates

28) How Do I Get Export Orders? Finding International Buyers

29) What Is APEDA In Import Export Business?

30) Which Is The Best Product To Export From India?

31)EXIM Remark by Manoj Kumar Faridabad

32)EXIM Remarks by Mahesh Telangana

33) What Licenses I Need To Start Import/ Export?

34) How Can I Increase My Import Export Business?

35) Which Is Best B2B Website For Import/Export Business?

36) Export Import Management with Global Marketing

37) How to Start Export Import Business | 51 Points Video

38) Scope for Commerce & Other Graduates in International Business
39)BE A SUCCESSFUL EXPORTER FOR OUR NATION - Marathi video
40) Export of Textile , Cotton, Agri., Food, & other products & services
41) Exports from MP, CG, MH, GJ & CA in Fresh Fruits & Vegetables
42) Exports in Agri. & Food Products- Hindi
43) Start your Online/E-Commerce Business
44) How to Start Export Import Business & Grow it
45) Exports in Textile & Other Products
46) Start and grow EXIM business - Live English Webinar
47)'Import Export Business!' Why, Who, What & How can one do it easily!!
48) Live: Export of Product & Services During & After Lock Down Period
49) Frauds in Import Export Business
50) Import Export for Business Man
51) Import & Export for Women
51) Import & Export for Graduate & Post - Graduate Students
52) Agriculture Exports from India
53) Digital Marketing Setup - Marathi
54)2nd Secret of Successful Businessman
55) Digital Marketing Set up
56) Legal Services Export / Export of Legal Services
57) Export & Import with UAE
58) Service Exports / Exports by Service Providers
59) Import Export Workshop/ Training/Course/ Diploma
60) Exports & Imports with USA
61) Selection on Product for Export
62) Top Products Exported from India
63) What to do import & export?
64)ABMM Career 2 - 'Careers in Business & Industries
65) How to do Import Export Business Successfully!'
66)5 Secrets of Successful Businessman
67) Export from MP, Chhattisgarh & Vidarbha Nagpur
68)EXIM Hindi - Textile & Apparel Export
69)EXIM Hindi - Export Import Practical Training In Delhi, Kolkata, Mumbai and Pune
70) Import Export Business
71) Import Export Business Hindi
72) Import Export Business English video

73) Import Export Business Marathi

74) Women in International Business by Exim Guru Adv. Jayprakash Somani

75) Opportunities in Foreign Trade- Adv. Jayprakash Somani's special interview

List Of Adv. Jayprakash Somani's Books

1. Supreme Court of India's Leading Case Laws on 'Insolvency & Bankruptcy Code 2016'

2. Bail Matters – Supreme Court's Latest Leading Case Laws

3. Arbitration Matters- Supreme Court's Latest Leading Case Laws

4. Property Matters - Supreme Court's Latest Leading Case Laws

5. Matrimonial Matters- Supreme Court's Latest Leading Case Laws

6. Election Matters- Supreme Court's Latest Leading Case Laws

7.SEBI Matters- Supreme Court's Latest Leading Case Laws

8. Banking Matters- Supreme Court's Latest Leading Case Laws

9. Service Matters- Supreme Court's Latest Leading Case Laws

10. Contempt of Court Matters- Supreme Court's Latest Leading Case Laws

11. Consumer Protection Matters- Supreme Court's Latest Leading Case Laws

12. Corporate Law- Supreme Court's Latest Leading Case Laws

13. Supreme Court's AOR Exam- Leading Cases

14. Armed Force Tribunal - Supreme Court's Latest Leading Case Laws

15. Acquittal From 376 - Supreme Court's Latest Leading Case Laws

16. Negotiable instrument – Supreme Court's Latest Leading Case Laws

17. Contract Act- Supreme Court's Latest Leading Case Laws

18. Insider trading- Supreme Court's Latest Leading Case Laws

19. Foreign Exchange and Management Act- Supreme Court's Latest Leading Case Laws

20. Income Tax Act- Supreme Court's Latest Leading Case Laws

21. Company Law- Supreme Court's Latest Leading Case Laws

22. Competition & Monopoly Matters- Supreme Court's Latest Leading Case Laws

23. Compassionate Appointment- Service Matters- Supreme Court's Latest Leading Case Laws

24. Compulsory Retirement- Service Matters- Supreme Court's Latest Leading Case Laws

25. Voluntary Retirement- Service Matters- Supreme Court's Latest Leading Case Laws

26. Removal/Dismissal/Termination from Service- Supreme Court's Latest Leading Case Laws

27. Seniority- Service Matter- Supreme Court's Latest Leading Case Laws

28. Promotion- Service Matter- Supreme Court's Latest Leading Case Laws

29. Equal Pay for Equal Work- Service Matter- Supreme Court's Latest Leading Case Laws

30. Condition of Service- Service Matter- Supreme Court's Latest Leading Case Laws

31. Customs Act- Supreme Court's Latest Leading Case Laws

These Books are available online at

1. **Notion Press:** https://notionpress.com/author/jayprakash_somani
2. **Amazon:** https://www.amazon.in/s?k=jayprakash+somani
3. **Flipkart:** https://www.flipkart.com/search?q=Jayprakash%20Somani

Printed by Libri Plureos GmbH in Hamburg,
Germany